Customer
Education

Claudia Gaillard Meer

Customer
Education

Nelson-Hall nh *Chicago*

LIBRARY OF CONGRESS CATALOGING IN PUBLICATION DATA

Meer, Claudia Gaillard.
  Customer education.

  Bibliography: p.
  Includes Index
  1. Customer relations. 2. Consumer education.

I. Title.
HF5415.5.M43   1984   658.8′12   84-6938
ISBN 0-8304-1049-X

Copyright © 1984 by Claudia Gaillard Meer

Manufactured in the United States of America

10 9 8 7 6 5 4 3 2 1

The paper in this book is pH neutral (acid-free).

Contents

Preface

Business and industry spend billions of dollars each year for education and training. Most of this training focuses on employee development, an area that has been studied, and is producing a growing literature. Employers also devote considerable resources to customer education, but almost no attention has been given to this subject.

The term *customer education* refers to any purposeful, sustained, and organized learning activity that is designed to impart attitudes, knowledge, or skills to customers or potential customers by a business or industry. It can range from self-instructional material for a particular product to a formal course related to a product or service. The educational activity is directly related to promoting sales or to assisting the customer in the use of the product or service. Customer education can occur before, during, or after a sale. It can also occur in the absence of a sale, as in situations where people participate in presale educational activity but do not purchase a product or service. Customer education, then, can be for customers or potential customers and it is often delivered in conjunction with the sale of a product or service.

Customer education is distinguished from consumer education in that the latter is usually provided by a third party, not the producer of the product being sold. The purpose of consumer education is to enable consumers to make more informed decisions on what product to purchase, not to promote the sale of a product.

Client education can be synonymous with customer education. The difference is one of context. The term *client* tends to connote a purchaser of a professional service, such as management consulting.

The general purpose of this study is to explore the nature and scope of customer education in business and industry today and to begin to broaden understanding of this phenomenon by examining specific programs in detail. A deeper understanding of customer education could aid the business community in improving this function in order better to serve its customers, society, and itself. It would also add to our understanding of an important and totally neglected aspect of adult education in the context of business and industry.

Special recognition is due my colleagues at Rutgers University, who provided constant encouragement and invaluable help, especially Gordon Darkenwald, Harold Beder, Harry Stark, William Weinberg, and Ernest Gross. I am also grateful to my husband, Richard, and my parents, Herman and Anita Gaillard, to whom this book is dedicated.

1
Overview of Customer Education

Virtually no research has been done on customer education, even though its existence appears to be widespread. Information in the area of customer education is limited to reports or case studies written by company personnel on particular customer training programs. No comparative or in-depth studies of customer education programs have been identified by the present researcher.

Exploratory research conducted by this investigator brought to light a fundamental question. If customer education is as widespread as it seems, why has it not been studied to any significant degree? It seems that the magnitude of customer education in business and industry has not been recognized. Although most companies offer some form of customer education, it is not usually a separately organized function within the company and therefore tends to have low visibility.

Not very much has been written about customer education. What is available primarily describes specific programs by specific companies and, for the most part, the articles appear in obscure periodicals. Customer service, according to Antuck and Wittnam (1965), represents one of the key competitive benefits that a company can offer in order to attract or keep business. However, books on the general topic of customer service only mention customer education; none discusses it in any detail. Yet, customer education is apparently widespread and has been in existence for a long time.

Education in Business and Industry

The knowledge base of industry-sponsored education and training is "precariously slim and fragmentary" (Smith, 1977:11). Attempts were made to study various aspects of education and training activities in business and industry by Lusterman (1977), Goldstein (1980), and Smith (1980). All three studies dealt with educational activities for employees. In addition, Wagner (1980), in his study of post-compulsory education and training, compared the cost of and funding for these activities, and looked at differences among participants in various types of programs.

One common area of agreement of these and other studies is that more education and training exists in private industry than has been acknowledged and more money is being spent on these activities than is being recorded.

> The lack of a coordinated information recording or reporting system, together with the reluctance of private industry to release such information to those outside the corporate structure, results in a great lack of knowledge regarding the extent of education and training opportunities within the private sector. [Stewart, 1980:33]

In a similar vein, Goldstein (1980, p.20) states:

> This is interesting in view of the millions of workers involved, the billions of dollars spent, and the hoped for effects on productivity, worker income, international competitiveness of the nation's economy, and equality of employment opportunity.

According to Smith (1980:10), employer-sponsored education

> takes many forms, employs an array of methods, and includes a wide range of content depending on the skills to be imparted and the purpose of the education. It ranges from the most informal training to highly formalized academic instruction.

Lusterman (1977:5) asserted that education and training activities derive from three needs, which are shared by all organizations. These are:

1. turnover and growth in personnel;
2. changes in the knowledge and skills required or available; and
3. a need to improve the skills and performance of present employees in their present jobs.[1]

He further states (1977:65) that the corporate education system has three characteristics that distinguish it from other education systems. These include:

1. high motivation of its participants;
2. the workplace as the setting for both learning and doing; and
3. the system as an instrument for achieving other goals, which include profit and growth.

Generalizing from his 22 percent response rate, Lusterman (1977) concluded that approximately 11 percent of the persons employed by firms with five hundred or more employees in 1974-1975 participated in in-house employer-sponsored courses during working hours. In addition, about 2 percent took company courses during nonworking hours. Seventy-five percent of all companies sponsored in-house courses for their employees, 89 percent offered tuition-aid or refund programs, and 74 percent allowed some employees to take outside courses during working hours. The larger the firm, the more likely it was to offer each type of program. Smaller firms primarily utilized outside resources for their training.

Lusterman (1977:12) estimated the direct expenditure for education and training in industry at about $2 billion for the companies in the category studied. This broke down to 80 percent for in-house activities, 11 percent for tuition aid programs, and 9 percent

---

1. From S. Lusterman, *Education in Industry,* 1977. Reprinted by permission.

for outside courses during working hours. The $2 billion represents an average of $60 per employee with the median company spending $16 per employee. This large difference is accounted for by the small number of high spending companies. Goldstein (1980) estimated an additional $1 billion in direct training costs for the rest of the private sector, plus about $2 billion in "lost time" salary costs for managerial and professional workers who received the bulk of training. Goldstein estimated a total training expenditure of approximately $10 billion (Goldstein, 1980:35). Wagner (1980:4,6) estimated that 7.4 million people received employer-sponsored education and training and that private industry spent $7.2 billion for classroom instruction at the job site.

In addition to discussing employee education and training, Lusterman (1977) included a brief section on educating nonemployees in his study. Included were data on customer education. Projecting from his 22 percent response rate from firms with five hundred or more employees, Lusterman estimated that 44 percent of the respondents provided some form of education to customers. The customers were usually the ultimate users of the instructing companies' products or services. The purpose of the education was primarily to teach skills and knowledge that were vital to the sale, maintenance, or use of the product. Lusterman also discussed customer education for a company's customer who performs essential roles for the provider's firm in connection with the manufacture, distribution, or servicing of its products. Some examples cited were:

1. Automobile manufacturers train their dealers.
2. Soft drink companies train their bottlers.
3. Food chains train their franchisees.
4. Insurance companies train their agents.

This type of customer education activity, when one company is the provider company's customer as well as its chief avenue to the consuming public, is exemplified in this report's case study of Hoffmann-LaRoche.

General Works Relating to Customer Education

Textbooks on customer service lack useful information on customer education. The purpose of one such book (Bender, 1976) is to examine the whole spectrum of a company's relations with its customers and to provide an overview of the customer service function, its scope and content. Yet the discussion on customer education is limited. Six basic functions of a customer service department are listed, one of which is technical services. Bender then mentions one part of the technical service function—customer training in the use of the company's products or services.

Buckner (1978) does something similar in his book. He places customer service into five categories, one of which is informational services. Like Bender, Buckner does not describe customer training in any detail. He only discusses lessons a store gives its customers.

This lack of information and emphasis on customer training is surprising given the apparent importance of customer education to a company. At a given price, demand for a product will vary with the extent and quality of service provided. Therefore, in determining the potential market for a product, it is necessary to describe the product in terms of its performance, price, and service. One aspect of service is customer education. Another reason for the importance of customer education (Bender, 1976:15) is that, for almost any company, it is more expensive to develop new customers than it is to maintain current ones. Customer education helps to provide the support needed to ensure that the product renders the promised service throughout its useful life; thus it helps to satisfy current customers and keeps them active with the company.

Bender (1976:1) defined customer service as "the set of activities performed in a company that interact with its customers, to insure their satisfaction with the company's products or services." He further stated that customer education should be conducted to insure proper use of the company's products, which can result in increased customer satisfaction and lower technical services costs. He saw determining the types of assistance a company will provide to help its customers maximize the benefits of using its products as a major marketing decision (1976:35). Therefore, customer education requirements should be related to their effect on the company's sales. An economic evaluation or cost/benefit analysis of customer education should be conducted. Neither Bender nor anyone else has discussed in detail this important area of evaluation.

Mansur (1977) discussed the need for professional continuing education for industrial marketers. He stated that the features, advantages, and benefits of industrial products and services can be positively conveyed in a continuing education program. The information provided often constitutes a review, renewal and reapplication of professional knowledge. First, programs should be delivered to a company's staff—the operations, sales, and customer service departments. Then, they should be provided to customers through sales and service calls, mail, seminars, publicity and advertising, or other industry communication channels.

McGuire (1973) stated that consumer complaints result from product misuse, improper maintenance, purchase of the wrong product for the intended purpose, and other failings or misunderstandings. Ciccolla (1969) concurred and added that manufacturers could do more to make the use and care of their products more easily understandable. Companies can do this in ways ranging from providing printed materials to offering formal courses. According to McGuire (1973) customer education programs have multiple purposes: to assist customers in making better purchase decisions in the first place; and to increase public awareness of products and services. He considered the latter purpose quasi-promotional. Examples given by McGuire of how some companies provide information to their customers include the following:

- Gillette Company: booklets on grooming, styling trends, clothes.

- Armstrong Cork Company: assistance with home remodeling and redecorating techniques.
- Pfizer Labs: booklet on symptoms and problems of venereal disease.
- Eastman Kodak: photographic consulting services.
- Hunt-Wesson Foods: menu-planning service.
- Singer: courses on sewing.
- Bristol-Myers: public health programs.
- Del Monte Foods: material on nutrition and menucards.[2]

Case Studies on Customer Education

Much that is written about customer education is in the form of case studies. One thing all the programs seem to have in common is that their main purpose is to increase sales. Antuck and Wittnam (1965) wrote case histories on applications of their company's product, a new form of polyethylene. The purpose of their customer education program was to gain acceptance for their product by offering free written information and a symposium on the product's uses to customers and potential customers. Polaroid's program, according to an article in *Business Week* (1960), consisted of instructional meetings for owners of Polaroid cameras. The company's rationale was that if people took good pictures with a Polaroid camera, they would use the camera more and therefore use more film. The company would also benefit from people showing good pictures to friends and relatives.

According to an article in *Industry Week* (1974), Parker-Hannifin Corporation opened a school in the early 1970s to let its customers know what it was doing in the fluid-power technology and equipment field. The school, which is still in existence, offers four continually running courses. The purpose of Parker-

2. From McGuire, *Consumer Affairs Department: Organizations and Functions*, 1973. Reprinted by permission.

Hannifin's program for its customers is to teach them how to maintain the equipment and keep it running properly. The Director of Training for the Fluidpower Group Training Department believes the school is successful because class registration is backlogged and many corporations have adopted the Parker courses to train their ever-changing work forces (Parker Fluidpower, 1978).

Towmoter Corporation in Cleveland is a maker of lift trucks (*Printer's Ink,* 1958). The company developed an instructional booklet for customers to insure better use of its product and therefore greater satisfaction from the product. Towmoter believes it gives its salesmen a new feature to open doors. Towmoter provides kits that contain complete materials for running a training school on the customer's premises. The kit includes an instructor's manual with a schedule for a three-day program. Each day consists of a theoretical discussion, a quiz period and discussion, and a demonstration period.

Devcon Corporation in Massachusetts invented a new product—"plastic steel" (*Printer's Ink,* 1962). The company then had the task of showing people how this product could restore damaged industrial equipment. They had to combat established industrial maintenance practices to show that restoring equipment is cheaper than replacing it. Regional sales managers and local sales representatives conducted meetings for customers, using demonstrations and slides showing various applications. They also conducted programs in high schools throughout the United States. They believe high school students are future customers and that this introduction familiarizes them with the company name and educates them to the principle of reducing maintenance costs by repairing with plastic steel. The company claims that this customer education program is the backbone of its sales effort, since its sales quadrupled after the first five years of the program. Devcon is one of the few companies that explicitly attributes increased sales to its customer training program.

Worthington Corporation (*Sales Management,* 1964) held practical classroom training sessions for its customers on the construction and maintenance of its diesel engines. The purpose of the training was to teach customers the best and most economical ways to attain maximum performance from the engines and how to care for the equipment. They primarily used working models for training. Having discontinued production of diesel engines, Worthington no longer conducts these sessions. However, formal training sessions are now held on the industrial air compressors manufactured by Worthington.

Rapids-Standard, Inc. (Jones, 1962), a materials handling company, has been conducting education programs since 1945 for customers and potential customers. They, like all the other companies discussed, use their program as a marketing tool to increase sales. In addition to increasing sales they believe it can bring about better understanding and cooperation between materials handling consultants and suppliers by finding better ways for both to work together toward more profit for the customer.

C. Arthur Weaver Company, Inc. (Larson, 1968), a power transmission specialist firm, built an educational center for new products, applications, and concepts. Salesmen invite participants to attend. Seminars address the following issues: what is new, how best to attack a problem and accomplish the highest net result for increased production, and how to achieve higher quality and less downtime and maintenance. The goal is increased sales, but this company feels education is the best way of accomplishing that goal and adding to the value of their place in the industry. ''The seminars have put us in a position of being the informed people in the area and as a result, industry turns to us for answers to its problems'' (Larson, 1968:53).

Larson (1968) also discusses the Womack Fluid Power Schools conducted by the Womack Machine Supply Company's education department. The Womack program, which began in 1968, is still in existence today. They have beginning and advanced classes and supply a three-volume text. Their program is used by over one hundred fifty fluid power distributors and many manufacturing firms, public schools, and colleges. Womack supplies texts, slides, instructor outlines, tests, diplomas, and advertising layouts. ''Our business has increased many times the national rate of our industry's growth. And, one of the biggest advantages is that service calls have been cut drastically" (Larson, 1968:53).

A bulletin published by Womack in 1977 discloses further information. In addition to the continental United States, classes are held in Hawaii, Canada, Australia, and other parts of the world. Distributors charge between $30 and $50 for the six-evening course with textbooks. "One secret to success is the tuition charge. Do not have a free school. It is hard to give away anything valuable, and people are prone to think it worthless." The bulletin further states that customers expect to receive a sales pitch at a free school, but expect to be taught on a nonproprietary basis in a school that they pay to attend. This statement corresponds with McGuire's statement that customer education activities are "too promotional" and do not have enough genuine "educational" content (McGuire, 1973:33).

Casting Engineers Company of Chicago (*Steel*, 1965) claims its customer education program was directly responsible for a series of new orders. The company developed a slide and flip chart presentation on the application of its products. In addition to increasing sales, the seminars helped to establish more areas of application for investment casting; and, due to greater customer familiarity with the process, the customer got new jobs off the ground with a minimum of trouble and afterservice.

Kodak (*Graphic Arts Monthly*, 1969) offers the same training program for its dealers, field representatives, and customers. The company started its classes in the 1940s at company headquarters in Rochester. In 1966, a Kodak Marketing Education Center staff was organized to help people keep up with the information explosion. In 1970, Kodak built an educational center on the outskirts of Rochester with satellite centers at the Kodak regional marketing headquarters. For people who cannot attend classes, the company developed an individualized communication and educational system called CAPAL—computer and photographic assisted learning. Interested persons can use CAPAL at any of the regional centers.

Autonetics, a division of North America Aviation, Inc., (Geiger, 1958) had a training course for potential customers on both its own computer and computers in general. This program was developed in 1958. The purpose of the training courses were fourfold:

1. to remove the mystery of computer operation for the uninitiated;
2. to help customers realize applications of computers in their own business;
3. to instruct customers in general programming and operation of their computers; and
4. to advance the applications of computers by making them more useful.[3]

Autonetics offered this course at its regional sales offices. The company also offered the course at a customer's location. Demonstrations, audio-visual material, sales brochures and operations manuals were used. They evaluated their programs, but they did not describe how nor provide the results of their evaluation efforts.

Varityper, a division of the Addressograph-Multigraph Corporation, located in East Hanover, New Jersey (*Editor and Publisher,* 1974) has a somewhat different customer education program. The company has eighty customer relations representatives stationed across North America in major cities to help customers with problems. They also have customers come to their home office in New Jersey for in-depth training on new machines. Customers also return for "follow up" sessions.

Digital Equipment Corporation (1978 and 1979) has an elaborate customer education program. Each year they publish a course catalog which is very specific and comprehensive. For example, the 1978 catalog has 239 pages. Each course is listed separately with a course abstract, prerequisites, course objectives, course outline, and course length. In addition to the courses offered at its regional education centers, the company provides on-site courses,

---

3. From R. F. Geiger, "Meeting to Turn Prospects into Customers," *Sales Management* (July 4, 1958). Reprinted by permission from *Sales & Marketing Management* magazine. Copyright 1958 Sales Management.

customized courses, and audio-visual courses. Approximately one hundred different courses are offered every year.

Waterbury Farrel Textron (*Training*, 1981), a manufacturer of complex heavy machine tools, uses videotape to pretrain its customers in the handling of these machines before and after they are delivered. The company started on this training venture in 1967 as a concomitant of its sales training program. To solve the problem of training a widely dispersed sales force, Waterbury Farrel purchased video equipment and taped presentations, given by district managers, on what the machine did and how it might solve a customer's problem. These tapes were sent to regional offices where the sales staff could look at them at their leisure. It became apparent that these tapes would be good selling tools, and sales representatives started using them on sales calls to back up their sales pitch. This led to the production of application sales tapes geared to individual companies. These tapes could be viewed at the customer's own facility or at one of Waterbury Farrel's facilities. They were used with both customers and potential customers. There was a charge for customized tapes; such tapes were valued by the customer in that they could be used for future training and retraining of operators.

Once a company purchased a piece of machinery, Waterbury Farrel loaned them video tapes and hardware. In this way, basic training was already well advanced by the time a customer's employees came to a Waterbury Farrel facility for personal instruction. Tapes were loaned for three months, along with appropriate playback equipment. After the three months, the customer could buy the tapes and the hardware.

Objectives

This study of customer education is essentially exploratory and descriptive. Its main objective is to explore the purposes, structures, processes, and outcomes of customer education in selected organizations. It was hoped that in-depth case studies would help to illuminate the basic dynamics of customer education programs and thus serve as a firm foundation for future research.

The following research questions served to guide the inquiry. They were suggested by a pilot study of several customer education programs in New Jersey.

1. What are the organization's objectives for customer education? These may include increasing product awareness and sales, reducing service calls, public relations, feedback for new product development, or new uses for a product, customer satisfaction, safety, and a legal obligation. Which of these objectives is most important under what circumstances? Is there one particular objective that is dominant for a particular kind of product?

2. What is the structure of customer education within a company? How does it operate? What is the relationship of customer education to employee education and to the sales function? How does the customer education function fit with other related company functions?

3. How is customer education organized and financed? Are the costs for customer education included in the price of the product or charged separately? How are costs determined?

4. Is customer education evaluated? To what extent? How? For what purpose?

5. What educational methods and materials are used for customer education? These may include lectures, demonstrations, simulations, audio-visual presentations, product literature, instruction manuals, and samples of products produced. How frequent is the use of each of these methods and under what circumstances and in what combination are they likely to be employed?

6. What are the major problems, issues, and questions for future inquiry?

Customer education takes place in many forms. A pilot study suggested that there is a continuum of customer education activities. At one end of the continuum are informal informational activities, including the provision of printed material, such as instructions that accompany a product or product literature. At the other end of the continuum are formal, organized educational activities, such as courses and seminars. Many of the activities that fall between these extremes of information giving and organized instruction are identified by this research.

2

Methodology

This study employed exploratory field research techniques to provide a comparative analysis of customer education programs in six major companies in the New York metropolitan area. The companies were chosen on the basis of their diversity and accessibility. An exploratory study was conducted because, when little is known about a problem such as customer education, this type of inquiry is particularly appropriate (Selltiz, 1976:92). The main purpose of an exploratory study is to gain familiarity with a phenomenon and to achieve new insights into it (Selltiz, 1976:90). According to Katz (Kerlinger, 1973:75), "exploratory studies have three purposes: to discover significant variables in the field situation, to discover relations among variables, and to lay the groundwork for later, more systematic and rigorous testing of hypotheses."

Selltiz (1976:92) states the methods she considers to be "especially fruitful" in exploratory research. These include: a review of the related studies; a survey of people who have had practical experience with the problem to be studied; and an analysis of "insight-stimulating" examples. She stresses the point that whatever methods are used they must be employed flexibly. All three of these methods were utilized in this research.

A pilot study was conducted to determine an appropriate approach to the study. Interviews were conducted with executives from eight companies in New Jersey and New York to gather information related to customer education activities. The companies and persons contacted are shown in table 2.1.

Table 2.1.
Company name and executive interviewed in first pilot study.

Company Name	Executive's Title
Bausch & Lomb, Inc.	Vice President, Sales Division
Eastman Kodak	Director, Advertising & Promotion
IBM	Marketing Manager
Meer Corporation	Executive Vice President
New Brunswick Scientific	Vice President, Marketing
Ortho Diagnostics	Supervisor, Educational Services
Siemens Corporation	Director of Training
W.R. Grace & Company	Director, Education and Training

These preliminary interviews were followed by telephone interviews and written correspondence with the executives involved with customer education activities at twenty New Jersey companies. The purpose of these supplementary contacts was to gain further knowledge about customer education activities in different types of companies. The companies and executives contacted are shown in table 2.2.

The eight companies selected for the initial stage of the pilot study were chosen because I was able to receive introduction to an individual in the company who in some way was familiar with the company's customer education activities. The second group of companies investigated in the preliminary research phase were chosen randomly from a list of companies in New Jersey with five hundred or more employees. Large companies were chosen be-

Table 2.2.
Company name and executive interviewed in second pilot study.

Company Name	Executive's Title
American Hoechst Co.	Group Director, Marketing Services
American Telephone & Telegraph	Manager, Customer Advice and Instruction
Automatic Data Processing	Division Vice President, Client Services
Automatic Switch Co.	Vice President, Advertising and Public Information
Bell Laboratories	Executive Director, Personnel and Education Division
Campbell Soup Co.	Director, Public Relations
Circle F Industries	Vice President, Sales
Curtiss-Wright Corp.	Corporate Training Manager
Fidelity Union Trust Co.	Executive Vice President
First National State Bank	Director of Communications
Ingersoll-Rand	Manager, Training
Lenox Inc.	Vice President, Advertising
New Jersey Bell	District Staff Manager, Community Relations
Perkin-Elmer	Director of Technical Training
Prudential Insurance Company	Senior Policyowner Service Consultant

Table 2.2. (continued)

Sandoz, Inc.	Coordinator, External Affairs
Tenneco Chemicals	Director of Marketing Services
The Great Atlantic & Pacific Tea Co.	Vice President, Executive Development and Training
Warner Lambert	Manager, Sales Training and Development
Western Electric	Public Affairs Manager

cause Lusterman (1977) found that the larger the company, the more likely it is to have organized educational programs.

The first group of eight interviews were conducted in person at company facilities, except for Eastman Kodak and Bausch & Lomb. In the case of these two companies, the interviews were conducted by telephone. At IBM and Ortho Diagnostics, I attended customer education classes and, in addition, I taught a class on adult learning as part of a customer education course at Ortho Diagnostics. For the second group of twenty companies, telephone calls were made to determine the person in charge of customer education activities. These were followed with a letter and brief questionnaire to the person so identified. (The questionnaire can be found in Appendix A.) Letters and questionnaires were sent to sixteen companies because three of the companies contacted, Bell Laboratories, Sandoz, and Western Electric, indicated that they did not sponsor any customer education activities. A representative of Campbell Soup wrote: ''Because of our limited staff— and the large volume of surveys, questionnaires and other research requests we receive—we simply cannot accommodate you in this instance.'' The sixteen companies to whom questionnaires were sent all responded.

Exploratory research was also conducted by contacting major organizations that presumably would have an interest in customer education. These were:

- American Society for Training and Development
- The Conference Board
- New Jersey Business and Industry Association
- New Jersey Chamber of Commerce
- National Association of Manufacturers
- Council for Noncollegiate Continuing Education
- New Jersey Manufacturers Association
- Employers Association of New Jersey
- New Jersey Office of Consumer Affairs
- National Association for Industry-Education Cooperation
- American Council on Education
- American Management Association

Not one of these organizations could supply information on customer education, although interest in the subject was expressed by most of them.

Case Studies

The data for this study were collected at six large companies in the New York metropolitan area, primarily through in-depth interviews with customer education personnel and customers who were receiving training. In addition, company and other relevant documents were analyzed and customer and train-the-trainer classes were observed. A combination of observation, interviewing, and documentary analysis was determined to be the best way to acquire maximum insight on the customer education activities in each organization (Clark, 1968:165). The companies studied were:

- Ortho Diagnostics, a division of Johnson & Johnson
- Varityper, a division of Addressograph Multigraph Corporation
- Digital Equipment Corporation
- Jersey Central Power & Light Company
- Merrill Lynch, Pierce, Fenner & Smith, Inc.
- Hoffmann-LaRoche, Fine Chemicals Division

Ortho manufactures scientific equipment for the health care field. Varityper manufactures phototypesetting equipment. Digital is a computer hardware and software company. Jersey Central Power & Light Company is a public utility. Merrill Lynch is an investment brokerage company and the fine chemicals division of Hoffman-LaRoche manufactures bulk vitamins.

A number of factors figured in the selection of companies for this study. First, the companies chosen were within commuting distance so I could visit each company several times without exorbitant travel expenses. This way, I could attend several training sessions and conduct interviews on several different occasions. Second, each company chosen was determined to have a unique characteristic that made it interesting to study.

Ortho was chosen because its customer education function was being reorganized at the time. Varityper had an extensive customer education train-the-trainer program. Digital was selected because it appeared to have the most extensive program of any company contacted. Jersey Central Power & Light, due to the nature of its product, had customer education that was more like consumer education. In addition, the company advocated decreased rather than increased use of its product by emphasizing energy conservation. Merrill Lynch was selected because a good portion of its customer education involved only potential customers. Hoffmann-LaRoche was chosen because its customers were not the final consumer of its product. Each company's customer education program was perceived to have at least one characteristic that made it unique.

Interviews

The initial data for this study were obtained through field interviews, held during the period February 1979 to May 1981. The first interview was held with the person in charge of the customer education unit. The interviews served two purposes. They allowed me to determine the structure of customer education activities in the organization and the names of the persons involved. They also enabled me to request and receive permission to interview these people.

After the initial interview with the head of the unit, I obtained interviews with other members of the department to obtain further information regarding customer education activities. Table 2.3 describes the positions of the persons who were interviewed at each company or in connection with the company's program. The personnel interviewed differed in their titles and responsibilities because the customer education function was organized differently in the various companies.

The interviews were unstructured and unstandardized. As Kerlinger (1973) suggests, when using this type of interview, the purpose of the research determines what questions should be asked. However, the researcher decides the content, sequence, and wording of the questions, depending upon the situation. This type of interview was deemed appropriate because of the exploratory nature of the study. Selltiz (1976:90) states that in exploratory studies, the research design must be flexible enough to permit the consideration of many different aspects of a phenomenon. Roethlisberger and the other researchers involved in the Hawthorne Studies often utilized unstructured interviewing and observation since these less structured methods allowed for maximum freedom of response and therefore resulted in a rich and diverse pool of data (Landsberger, 1968:94).

Table 2.3.
Companies studied and titles of persons interviewed.

Merrill Lynch, Pierce, Fenner & Smith, Inc.	Jersey Central Power & Light Company
Local office vice-president Investor information specialist Sales manager Local office manager Two account executives Staff attorney, Securities and Exchange Commission Senior interpretive specialist, N.Y. Stock Exchange	Customer relations manager Home energy savings program assistant, N.J. Department of Energy Home energy savings program manager, N.J. Department of Energy Manager of consumer services
Ortho Diagnostics	Hoffmann-LaRoche
Education coordinator/ Manager of technical resources Education coordinator/ Sales representative Manager educational services/Blood bank product manager Manager of technical literature Customers	Director of vitamin communications Regional sales manager Customers Vitamin advisory board member

Table 2.3. (continued)

Varityper	Digital
Two technical support representatives	Marketing manager, Educational services
Branch manager	Corporate manager, Educational services
Several marketing support representatives	Sales vice-president
Sales specialist	Training center manager
National sales manager	Field service training representatives
Technical support manager	Customers
Vice-president of sales	

Interviews were held in the office of the interviewees, in classrooms, in lunchrooms, and over the telephone. The duration of the field interviews varied in length from one to four hours. Telephone interviews generally lasted one-half hour. At least two interviews were held with the head of the customer education unit. The initial interviews have already been described. The second interviews were held after the field work was completed to review what was learned and to insure that all topics concerning the companies' customer education activities were discussed. In addition, when the write-up of a company was completed, a copy of the report was sent to the head of the customer education unit to review for accuracy and to determine if any important points were overlooked. The case reports were subsequently revised on the basis of these comments.

When approached for interviews, the interviewees in all but one case were cooperative. They seemed to be flattered that their company's program was chosen for study. Also, since customer education is not an area that has been previously studied, for most of these people it was a new and possibly pleasurable experience to be interviewed. I first explained the purpose and objectives of the research. Then the method by which the interviewee and his or her company was selected was described. Next, I identified the research as being part of a scholarly study and explained how it related to my occupation. The next step was to ask questions designed to develop an active interest on the part of the interviewee. These questions are categorized as rapport builders (Festinger, 1966:335,354). When these preliminaries were taken care of, I began the questioning on the customer education program. The interviews were recorded by note taking and on occasion by using a tape recorder.

Participant Observation

According to Bruyn (1970:284), a researcher must become highly aware of his subject and its surroundings in order to obtain an accurate intuitive grasp of it. One way to do this is through participant observation. A participant observer lets variables define themselves in the context of the research. Pearsall (1970:341) states that participant observation involves the field worker utilizing visual observation and interviewing to get data from live subjects. Zelditch (1970:220) states that participant observation occurs when the field worker directly observes and also participates in the sense that he has durable social relationships in a group or organization. He or she may or may not play an active part in events.

I observed at least one customer training session conducted by each company and a train-the-trainer session at one company. At these sessions, conversational interviews were held during breaks and after class sessions with the instructors and the customers in training. I was introduced to each class at the start of the program by the instructor, and I briefly described my research objectives to the class. I did not participate in class discussions. Information was recorded by note taking and in most cases was supplemented by using a tape recorder. Whenever possible, I sought to clarify points and to ask questions the same day they arose by speaking to the instructors and the customers as soon as the class recessed. Information obtained from these informal interviews was recorded as soon as I took my place in the classroom again.

Participant observation made it possible to check assertions against facts. By noting discrepancies, I became aware of some distortions made by the persons interviewed (Becker, 1966:139). For example, in one case study, an interviewee told me that one benefit of bringing customer trainers to their headquarters for train-the-trainer classes was to enable them to meet the staff with whom they had had only phone contact. However, when this person came to one of the classes to make a few remarks, he never introduced himself and several of the participants did not know who he was.

Finally each company studied had brochures and other information describing its customer education activities. This material was readily available, as were handout materials distributed at training sessions. This provided a general description of what was going on and was helpful in raising questions on specific aspects of each activity. Annual reports for each company were read, as were Dunn and Bradstreet reports, to get a better picture of the company as a whole.

The next six chapters present the data gathered during my study of customer education activities in the six companies from 1979 to 1981. Each case study begins with a brief description of the company and goes on to describe the customer education program. Included is a description of how customer education functions fit into the overall structure of the company and how customer education activities are organized; the company's objectives for customer education and their relative importance; how customer education is financed; the educational methods and materials used for customer education; and major problems and concerns as perceived by customer education personnel.

The cases are presented in the order in which the field work proceeded. Varityper is described first, followed by Ortho Diagnostics, Digital Equipment Corporation, Jersey Central Power & Light Company, Merrill Lynch, Pierce, Fenner & Smith, and Hoffmann-LaRoche.

3

Varityper

Varityper, a division of the Addressograph-Multigraph Corporation employs twelve hundred persons and has thirty-eight branches in the United States, with its home office located in East Hanover, New Jersey. The company manufactures type composition equipment for worldwide sale. Specifically, they manufacture machines for the composition of body copy and display type, including high speed automated phototypesetting equipment and video editing terminals for in-plant, commercial graphic arts, and publishing markets. At the time of my investigation, Varityper manufactured three series of phototypesetting machines: the Comp/Set, the Comp/Edit, and the 4800 series. Each machine had several models that vary according to their capabilities.

This case study involved interviewing the head of the marketing department, two technical support representatives, the national sales manager, the branch manager in Mountainside, New Jersey, and several marketing support representatives (MSRs). Additionally, I attended several train-the-trainer classes for marketing support representatives.

As is the case with most technical equipment, training is needed in order to operate a phototypesetter properly. To meet this educational need, Varityper has established a customer training function, conducted by the marketing department. How this department fits into the overall structure of Varityper is shown in figures 3.1 and 3.2.

Figure 3.1.
How customer training fits into the Varityper organization.

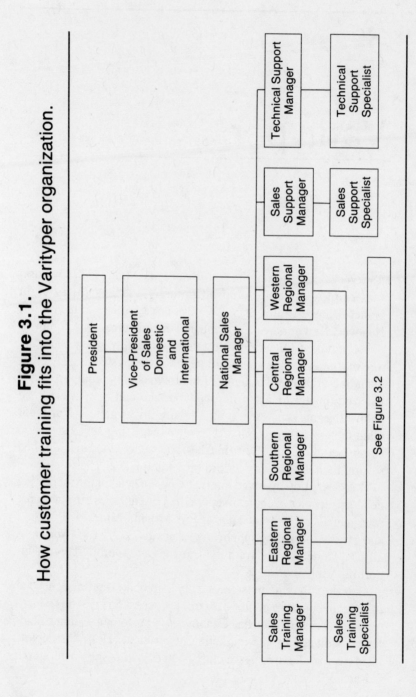

The home office sales department consists of two sales support staffs: sales specialists and technical support representatives. Sales specialists write material to aid the sales force and put into writing various applications for which the machines can be used by potential customers. In other words, their primary function comes before the sale. Technical support representatives train the customers to operate the equipment. Their primary function comes after the sale. Both the sales support manager and the sales training manager report to the national sales manager. There is no linkage between employee training, which is part of the personnel department, and customer training, which is part of the marketing department.

There are approximately one hundred twenty MSRs worldwide. A description of the major requirements and job responsibilities of an MSR follows:

Figure 3.2.
How MSRs fit into the Varityper organization.

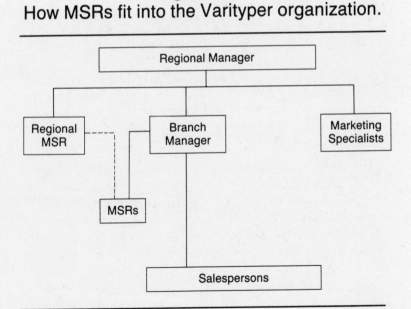

1. develops a working knowledge of the operation of product equipment and learns about basic business and customer relations.
2. attends formal skill training programs that develop knowledge of marketing policies and practices (these are the "train-the-trainer" classes).
3. performs demonstration and training assignments on basic equipment under direct and indirect supervision.
4. develops a knowledge of basic business practices and customer relations that enable the sale and proper application of product equipment.
5. maintains effective relationships with customers and fellow employees.
6. develops and updates knowledge of competitors' equipment.
7. establishes and updates a file of manuals and offers product "literature" to maintain product familiarity.

This description was given by the technical support specialist to MSRs in a training class and is on file in the Varityper personnel office. It is not a complete listing of all the duties of the MSR, only the major job responsibilities. The description further states:

Applicants should be self-motivated and have the ability to plan and organize their time and have an acceptable driving record. Candidates must be willing to travel and work unusual hours as needed; be able to communicate well and be prompt and dependable.

The MSRs are stationed across the continental United States in the branch offices. Additionally, there are MSRs in Canada, in Hawaii and overseas, including Africa and Holland. The MSRs abroad conduct training for Varityper's eighty subsidiaries and one hundred dealers. The MSRs in the United States report to the branch manager where they are stationed and communicate with the regional MSR.

A regional MSR supervises and advises the MSRs in his or her region. There is one regional MSR in the Northeast, one in the

South, one in the Midwest, and one on the West Coast. The MSRs have a high level of autonomy. They set schedules for training and follow the most efficient travel pattern. An MSR controls the training level needed for each customer. Unless there is a problem, the MSR, along with the customer, adapts the training to the application involved. MSRs also aid salespersons in their branch by giving demonstrations to potential customers on the various equipment. Also, and increasingly in the branch offices that are large enough to have a good sized demonstration area, the MSR conducts some of the customer training right there.

The primary responsibility of a MSR is to give the customer the initial training on the purchased machine and to help the customers with any problems they may encounter. This can prove to be a difficult task since many of the MSRs cover large districts. For instance, the MSR stationed in Denver, Colorado, has to cover eighteen hundred miles, from Utah to Texas, including parts of nine different states. This is why the MSR staff is expanding fairly rapidly. Until recently, the MSRs would train the operators individually. Now, MSRs hold classes for three or four persons at a time. Aside from saving money for Varityper and the customer, this also saves valuable time.

The cost of the customer training is included in the price of the phototypesetter. Varityper's policy is that they will train any two people the customer wants anytime during the first ninety days after the system is installed. The training is conducted until it is finished, which usually takes three to seven days. The length of the training generally depends upon the complexity of the system purchased and the experience of the operators. The completion of training is determined jointly by the MSR and the customer. After the initial training, the MSR will visit the customer at the end of four, eight, and twelve weeks. The MSR's job is to keep a phototypesetter with the purchaser. So, he or she teaches the operator not only to use the equipment but also to like the system. The customer knows an MSR is always as near as the phone if any problems arise.

If more training is needed than can fit into the initial ninety-day period, or if the customer wants to train more than two people, the MSR will do so. Generally, the branch manager decides whether or not to charge for extra training or retraining. If the customer is a good one and/or the manager thinks the customer may buy another machine, there will be no charge. However, if the reason the customer needs additional training is primarily his own doing, Varityper will charge for the training. For example, one customer in Texas had a rapid turnover of operators, primarily because his pay scale was below that of other companies in the area. So, after the MSR trained five new operators for this customer, Varityper started charging for the additional training. According to one branch manager, good customer relations are essential for maintaining and increasing sales, so it is imperative that discretion be used in making such decisions. Should the branch manager decide to charge for training, the guideline suggested by Varityper is $100 per day if the MSR goes to the customer and $75 per day if the customer goes to the branch office for the training.

The MSR fills out a customer contact report for each customer, which is filed both at the branch office and New Jersey headquarters with the technical support specialists in the marketing department. This report discusses every aspect of the training that takes place after the installation of the machinery, including who was trained and for how long. This serves as a reminder to the MSR when he or she makes the follow-up calls or is called back for retraining. MSRs train so many customers that it is difficult for them to remember the particular problems of each customer or operator. Sometimes a company does not want to spend any or much time on training because the owner wants to see results immediately from his expensive investment. If this happens, the MSR is instructed to try to be firm and insist on proper training. This is one of the points stressed in MSR training class when discussing the importance of customer training. The MSR will remind the owner that he just spent $30,000 or $40,000 for a machine, and if it is to work the way it should, operators need training.

Sometimes a problem arises when a customer's operator is not trainable. The technical support manager estimates that this happens three to five times per year. It is usually because the operator has no experience on anything similar to a phototypesetter. If this happens, the MSR is instructed to consult with the branch manager on what to do. Their choices are twofold: either continue trying to train or suggest to the customer that he hire another operator. The latter is often difficult to do, because in many of the smaller companies that purchase a machine, the operator is a relative of the owner. However, it is up to the branch manager to handle the situation and decide what to do since the MSR's primary mission is to support and assist the sales and marketing functions of the company. If the MSR and branch manager determine that an operator is not trainable, it is possible that the customer will decide he does not want the system. This does not happen often, but when it does, it is money out of the salesperson's pocket. Therefore, the MSR cannot make this decision alone. MSRs are continually told that almost everything they do affects present and future sales, so they should consult their branch managers whenever possible before making major decisions.

Another problem that occasionally arises is when the salesperson undersells a customer. When an MSR goes to a customer to train the operators, he or she may find that the machine does not have the capacity to do what the customer wants it to do. Salespersons attribute this to the fact that the persons who purchase the machine for the company often do not know or understand what the company intends to use the machine for. So, when given the choice between several models with different capabilities, most customers will choose the least expensive model, which is also the least sophisticated.

Two potential problems between the MSR and the sales representative came to light during the discussions. The first is that the salespersons often ask the MSRs to do demonstrations. This is definitely part of the MSR's job function. However, often the MSR has a training session planned during the time the salesperson scheduled a demonstration. So, the salesperson often has to reschedule the demonstration. Sometimes this creates a problem because the salespersons feel that the MSR's first responsibility is to help them with sales, so if demonstrations are what they need at the moment, the MSR should do them. In these situations the branch manager must make the decision.

The other problem that came up during my interviews at Vari-typer was in the distribution of documentation. The home office sends technical support bulletins to the MSRs dealing with problems that occur on the machines as these are brought to the attention of the home office. Approximately one hundred of these bulletins are written each year by the technical support specialists in the home office and sent to the MSRs at the branch offices. However, many MSRs were not receiving these bulletins, so the home office now sends the bulletins to their homes. When the bulletins are too large to fit in the average sized mailbox, the home office sends a mailgram to the MSR at home telling him or her to expect a bulletin in the office. This way, if the MSR does not receive the bulletin, he or she can go to the branch office and ask for it. In speaking about these bulletins to the MSRs in their training class, the technical support specialist in charge of the Comp/Set machine said:

> You [the MSR] are entitled to have it [the bulletin]. If anyone in the branch should have it, you should have it. You are the ones who are out in the field training these people to operate the system the sales representative has sold. They sell it. The only problem is to sell them the right system for their needs. Then it's all on your shoulders. And it's a very big job. You have to be a very responsible person. You have to know all the answers or at least know where to go to get them. Which brings me to the regional MSRs. If you have a problem, it's best to check with the regional MSR first. . . . Try to talk to the regionals first. Then call me. If you have a problem you can't talk to your manager about or your regional MSR, call me. If you have a personality problem, call me. We had several MSRs quit because their manager wouldn't listen. Well, the managers have an awfully big job to do. They are not only in charge of all the MSRs, they are in charge of all the sales. They are very busy. In a way, it's a compliment they forget about you. You do such a good job, they don't have to worry about what's going on.

Varityper has a well-organized "train-the-trainer" program for their MSRs. The marketing specialists take the same training to learn how to operate the system in order to better advise the salespeople how to sell it. These sessions are conducted by the technical support specialists, of which there are currently three. Each technical support specialist deals with the operation of one line of machinery. He or she conducts the training session on the machine, serves as the resource person for the MSRs, and writes the technical support bulletins on a particular machine. The technical support specialists all had worked as MSRs. This is how they receive their training on the machines. Every new MSR attends a course on each machine at Varityper's New Jersey headquarters.

I attended several sessions of the course on the Comp/Set machine. The course ran for two weeks. The teaching methods employed were demonstration and practice, with some lecture and discussion. Some homework was given. Highly technical jargon was used by both the instructor and the students. The first day was devoted to an orientation to the course and preliminary lectures. The rest of the course involved practice on the machines. Enough machines were set up in the classroom so that there were no more than two persons per machine. If possible, a relatively new person was paired up with a more experienced person. The students learned how to fix minor problems without the aid of servicemen as well as operate the machine. Sometime during the course, the class took a tour of the factory.

The materials used during the course were a notebook and an operating and reference manual. The instructor stressed the use and importance of the notebook for future reference, since information is written in the student's own words. At the start of the course, everyone introduced themselves. In my class there were thirteen participants from all over the United States. Their length of employment with Varityper ranged from three weeks to seven months. Most had had no typesetting work experience prior to their employment at Varityper. All of the MSRs were college graduates and many came from graphic arts schools. Their backgrounds were in areas such as fine arts, design, business, communication arts, anthropology, accounting, sales, and graphic arts. The course instructor, as is the case with the other technical support specialists, was an MSR before being promoted to her current position. This is worth noting as it demonstrates that there is a career path for these customer trainers. One promotion possibility would be to technical support specialist. Another would be to regional MSR or branch manager. There are four regional MSRs and thirty-eight branch managers. After eighteen months, an MSR can be promoted from MSR II to MSR I. The job is the same, but the salary is higher.

The instructor encouraged the participants to interrupt her for questions at any time. She noted that she had a typesetting machine in her office so if an MSR had a specific question, he or she could call the instructor. She would then turn to her machine, and answer the question immediately.

After this introduction, a written review quiz was given. Before the MSRs came to New Jersey for the course, they were sent material to study, and this is what they were tested on. The instructor does not waste valuable time on information that can be learned through self-study. The quiz lasted forty-five minutes and contained seventy-four short questions. If an MSR did poorly on the quiz, he or she was asked to leave the course and go back to the branch office. They were given one more chance to take the exam and attend the course. The pass rate on the exam was 90 percent.

After the quiz, the national sales manager made a few remarks and greeted everyone individually. He was friendly and asked each MSR about his or her territory. He discussed the importance of MSR training "as an opportunity to bear down without others [salesmen, customers] breaking down your concentration. Class is an opportunity to concentrate outside of the hectic branch."

The national sales manager also mentioned that the company had planned to upgrade the MSR training to include additional sessions to introduce new developments or major changes in a system. He added that the advantage Varityper has over its competitors is that it offers its free customer training on a timely basis. Competitors charge for their training and often the customers have to wait months for it. "Varityper's 'follow-up' is considered to be the only one so extensive in its field." The instructor stated that when she worked for one of the competitor's training operators, the only training she received was from the servicemen, and this was primarily trial and error.

A training program is set up when approximately ten MSRs require training. In other words, a class is established when the need is demonstrated. When an MSR needs training or retraining, the regional MSR or branch manager will call the appropriate technical support specialist at the New Jersey headquarters. When the technical support specialist has enough names, she sets up the training program and confirms it with the participants. An expense check is then sent to the participants to cover airfare, ground transportation, and dinners. Lunch and breakfast are served at Varityper and the hotel arrangements are also made by the company. Each MSR must complete a self-paced instructional program before going to the training session. This is what they are tested on during the first day of the program. Since a class cannot always be set up when it is needed, the MSR gets enough training at the branch to enable him or her to work immediately. The branch manager or another MSR will give this initial training. Also, there is some trial and error learning.

At the time of this study, approximately one MSR training program was held each month. This was because the MSR staff was expanding, and there was quite a bit of turnover. Some MSRs went into sales because they could earn more money there. Others left for personal reasons, often because they did not want to travel and be away from their families so much. The MSRs in the class this researcher attended were all female (there were only a handful of male MSRs) and the majority were in their twenties. On the average, an MSR stays with Varityper in that capacity for three to five years. An MSR receives a car, expense account, and charge card, and is allowed 375 personal miles per month on the car. An MSR is paid for a forty hour week and compensated for overtime.

At no time during the training were the MSRs taught *how* to teach the customer to use the machine. In other words, they were not taught any instructional techniques. They were taught only the technical knowledge and skills needed to operate the phototypesetting equipment. The MSRs were repeatedly told that the salesperson sells the machine to customers; the function of the MSR is to make the operator like the machine. It seemed logical to me that the MSRs could use some training on how to teach. When I suggested this, it was agreed that teaching skills should be part of the MSRs' training and that in the future, the classes would include teaching procedures.

The MSRs' work is not formally evaluated. However, Varityper takes into consideration the fact that some customers cannot be trained. They cannot grasp how to use the machine. If a customer does not learn or seems as if he does not want to learn, the MSR talks to the branch manager about it. Varityper is currently thinking about instituting a procedure whereby customers sign a statement that describes the training they received and states that they were satisfied with the training. The company hopes this will prevent some customers from claiming the training was inadequate or incomplete.

The train-the-trainer classes are formally evaluated. The instructor evaluates each MSR after the training sessions. She discusses her evaluation with each participant, and then sends a written report to his or her branch manager.

Varityper has a defined customer education program within its sales department. The program is well organized and fairly extensive. A lot of resources are devoted to training both customers and trainers. These resources seem to be well spent. Varityper appears to take pride in this program and is eager to improve it.

4

Ortho Diagnostics, Inc.

Ortho Diagnostics, Inc., a subsidiary of Johnson & Johnson, with headquarters and manufacturing facilities in New Jersey and Texas, has a customer education program that is in a state of flux. Ortho provides blood banks and clinical laboratories with products to analyze components of blood and other body fluids as an aid in medical diagnosis. Their products include blood grouping and typing sera, Rh vaccine, and reagents to determine cervical malignancy, pregnancy, serum hepatitis, and infectious mononucleosis.

During the one and one-half year period in which I conducted this study, customer education at Ortho underwent a major organizational change. Accordingly, this case study will be divided into three sections: prereorganization, reorganization, and postreorganization.

Prereorganization Period

Early in 1979, when this study was begun, Ortho had an educational services department that conducted all the company's customer education programs. At the time, the educational services department had five members—one manager, one program coordinator, and three education coordinators—all based at the New

Jersey facility. The program coordinator was responsible for all the clerical work in the department. The education coordinators were medical technologists.

The department had several functions. It offered courses in applied blood banking, case study clinics in immunohematology, workshops in educational technics, the Ortho Institute of Laboratory Management, and seminars and workshops at local institutions.

On the average, the staff offered eleven one-week "schools" each year and additional short workshops. The course in applied blood banking was offered four times per year, twice in New Jersey, once in California, and once in Texas. The workshop in educational technics was offered once each year in New Jersey, and the Ortho Institute of Laboratory Management was offered three times each year, twice in New Jersey and once in Texas. The scheduling varied according to the demand in a particular year.

These courses were taught by the educational services staff or by outside professionals. For example, I taught an adult learning section in one of the educational technics workshops. Participants came from all over the country to attend these workshops. The educational services staff also wrote books and articles, self-instructional packages, and a case-in-point series, a group of case studies that were accompanied by separate answer booklets. The educational services department also developed all the materials for lectures, including class outlines and slide presentations. In addition, the educational coordinators trained the sales representatives to train customers in the use of Ortho products.

Ortho did not provide its instructors with training in education techniques. Instructors were given certain topics on which to speak and they gave presentations with very little guidance from the company. However, most of these presentations were made by the educational services staff, who repeated these workshops and were thereby somewhat experienced in teaching. The outside professionals who were employed were either experienced teachers or consultants.

Tuition for the short workshops, the course in applied blood banking, and the case study clinic was free for customers and po-

tential customers. However, there was a $300 tuition charge for
the Institute of Laboratory Management and the educational technics workshop because the company held that total subsidy could
not be justified for programs not entirely related to Ortho products. The fee included breakfasts, lunches, graduation banquet,
coffee breaks, and all educational materials. It did not include
transportation, lodging, and dinners. If the classes were held at an
Ortho facility or a place other than a hotel, transportation between
the hotel and the classroom facilities was also included. The fee
only partially covered Ortho's expenses. A former education coordinator, who became a sales representative, estimated that the
fee covered only 50 percent of Ortho's expenses. The company
subsidized the remaining amount. The classes were kept small,
with an average of fifteen to twenty participants per program. Another former education coordinator, who became the manager of
technical resources in the immunodiagnostics division of technical
services, said that a class was given only if there were at least
twelve persons.

The Ortho Institute of Laboratory Management was specifically
designed for laboratory managers, laboratory supervisors, or
chief technologists responsible for personnel and fiscal management of hospital laboratories. Participants were asked to have at
least one year of experience in a supervisory position as a prerequisite for the course. The program in New Jersey was conducted
by a faculty team comprised of management educators and specialists from the Institute of Management and Labor Relations'
Management Education Department at Rutgers University. When
the program was conducted in Texas, the faculty were from the
University of Texas at Dallas; in California, the faculty were from
the University of California at Irvine.

The manager of the former educational services department at
Ortho coordinated this program. (He became a blood bank product manager at Ortho when the reorganization took place.) The
program was based on the concept that, to gain optimum benefit,
the individual must actively participate in an educational experience. Accordingly, the sessions were informal and included much
small group activity. The course consisted of lectures, role play,

case studies, and competitive learning activities—all used to illustrate the principles of management. The objectives of the program
were: to broaden the participants' knowledge of management the-
ory and practice, to improve interaction skills of employees in
communication and motivation, to enhance leadership effectiveness in decision making, and to insure understanding of the duties
and responsibilities of management. All the problems discussed in
the program related directly to hospital laboratory management
and were written by the members of the educational services department at Ortho.

The participants in the four different one-week courses were
primarily recruited with a direct mail campaign, though sales representatives also recruited participants. According to one of the
former education coordinators, there were approximately six
thousand hospitals in this country in 1979 and each hospital had
one blood bank with at least one supervisor. This was and is
Ortho's primary market. This market also extends worldwide, but
educational services worked abroad only occasionally. A general
pamphlet was sent out containing the educational services calen-
dar for a particular year with the name, date, and location of the
programs. A flyer for each individual one-week program was also
sent out.

In-field programs were (and are) a part of the customer education function at Ortho. Before 1980, between seventy and ninety
were conducted each year, generally by the sales representatives
with the assistance of the educational services staff. Educational
services informally trained the sales representatives in teaching
techniques and also provided them with all their instructional material, including class outlines and audiovisual material. They also
provided samples for the in-field workshops. Tuition was free for
customers. A former education coordinator estimated that in 1979
these workshops cost Ortho $1,000 a day if taught by someone on
the educational services staff and $600 a day if taught by a sales
representative. The difference was accounted for by travel expenses. The sales representatives determined who came to the

workshops, because they used the workshops to get more business (potential customers) or to solidify present business (present customers).

One type of in-field program was the "wet" workshop. These workshops were elementary courses in applied science for customers and potential customers and included laboratory work. The format consisted of lecture, discussion, and demonstration. They were generally conducted by someone on the educational services staff with the assistance of the local sales representatives. The sales representatives usually decided which customers would be invited to attend the workshops. The workshops were given free of charge to Ortho customers. Ortho sponsored these workshops to build sales.

The other type of in-field programs conducted by educational services were the "dry" workshops. These consisted of lecture and discussion but included very little, if any, laboratory work.

The educational services department also developed literature and educational aids. Their publications list in 1979 included twenty-nine seminar reports and timely topics, sixteen books and pamphlets, four education brochures, four films, eight charts, numerous self-instructional packages, and miscellaneous publications including periodic newsletters on different topics. The editor, who was located in the marketing department, indicated that she "reviewed and edited all publications to make sure they met the company posture. This was an unwritten rule." In addition, she wrote several publications herself. The primary ones were "Blood Lines," a newsletter issued four times each year, and "Reference Points," a two-sided sheet that summarized salient practical points and indicated where to go for more information. The editor also promoted particular product lines via brochures and bulletins for the sales force. Customers were not charged for most of the publications.

Although most of this material was free, Ortho established a price for everything. The primary reason for this, as stated by a former education coordinator, was for the "customer's valuation.'' The customer felt well treated when he did not pay for an item that he knew had a certain dollar value. The secondary reason for establishing a price was to permit charging people who were not customers. However, most of the material was distributed to customers. All publications were listed in a pamphlet entitled "Current Publications," which was distributed to all Ortho customers.

In a sense, customers were paying for these materials and the so-called free training programs. According to a former education coordinator, Ortho products were more expensive than their competitors' products. One reason was that their competitors did not supply their customers with training programs and material. She further stated that "Ortho is a company known for its services and they want to keep this reputation. Service is the number one thing and customer education is part of service." Another former education coordinator felt that educational services helped their sales, despite the resulting higher prices. It was noted that sometimes people took Ortho's services for granted and would switch to a competitor's product when they realized they were able to purchase a similar quality product at a lower cost. Then they would call one of the education coordinators and ask why they no longer were contacted for workshops and no longer received material. More often than not, they would switch back to Ortho products. Ortho consciously used its customer training to attract and keep customers. This was a Johnson & Johnson philosophy and was the subject of their 1977 annual report.

One type of publication that Ortho put together and distributed was its self-instructional packages. For example, one package was called "Resolution of Cell Problems Encountered in Autoimmune Hemolytic Anemia." This learning tool for entry-level medical technologists was developed by one of the education coordinators. The package was presented as a folder containing a filmstrip with a fold-up viewer and a programmed instruction booklet. The inside cover contained the filmstrip and viewer with instructions for use. It also presented instructions for the use of the package, including the time it should take to complete it. The inside cover also stated in bold letters, "Through continuing education, scientific discovery becomes applied patient care. At Ortho Diagnostics we are committed to participate in discovery and to provide continuing education for the medical community."

The directions on the self-instructional package started out by stating the prerequisites for effectively using the package. Then followed the objectives of the package and how to use it. The individual shots on the filmstrip were numbered to coordinate with paragraphs in a booklet. At the end of the booklet was a final quiz, followed by the answers. Several blank pages were left for notes. The package was priced at $20. However, Ortho customers received the package free of charge.

The Ortho sales representatives lectured at schools that offered a curriculum in medical technology. They wanted the students, the people who would be using their products in the future, to be familiar with Ortho products. Ortho reasoned that if these students had anything to say about which products should be purchased at their places of employment, they would be more likely to choose Ortho's products because they were accustomed to using them. The educational services department developed the material for these programs. Approximately ten were conducted each year.

According to a former education coordinator, Ortho's major problem in providing customer education programs was the lack of a model for validating the program. They needed a reliable way to evaluate the sales impact of their efforts to justify their budget to Ortho's top management. An effort was made by the former manager of educational services to do this. He pulled out all the accounts that showed increases in sales. Then he separated these accounts into those that received training and those that did not. He concluded that there were 14 percent more customer accounts with training and sales increases than with sales increases and no training. Sales representatives claimed, however, that this study was not valid. Although the sales representatives worked well with educational services, their sentiment was that their efforts increased sales, not the efforts of the educational services department. A method was needed to identify the effect of the training programs on sales.

Reorganization Period

At the end of 1978, Dr. R. G. Nadeau became president of Ortho. He held the belief that Ortho personnel should not be centralized at their headquarters in Raritan, New Jersey; rather, personnel should be spread into the regional offices as much as possible. As part of this reorganization, educational services was disbanded by the end of 1979. The education function was shifted to five technical specialists, one for each regional center (see figure 4.1). At the time, there were five centers: Bridgewater, New Jersey; Atlanta, Georgia; Chicago, Illinois; Arlington, Texas; and Irvine, California.

In the beginning of 1980, Dr. Nadeau left Ortho and Fred A. Espinosa took charge as company group chairman. A decision was then made to consolidate the regional centers in three locations— New Jersey, Texas, and Illinois. Top management also felt that the regional centers should function less autonomously, and more emphasis should be placed on a central administration. This meant that while many people would remain in the regions, they would receive their technical direction from company headquarters in Raritan. This way, all company personnel who provided educational and/or technical assistance to customers would report to the director of technical services and, therefore, any information they gave to their customers would reflect a uniform company policy. The manager of technical literature described this policy in the following way: ''We all communicate our message to the customer with the same philosophy.''

As of late fall 1980, the technical specialists were still dispersed in five locations although the regions had been consolidated to three. The manager of technical resources in the immunodiagnos-

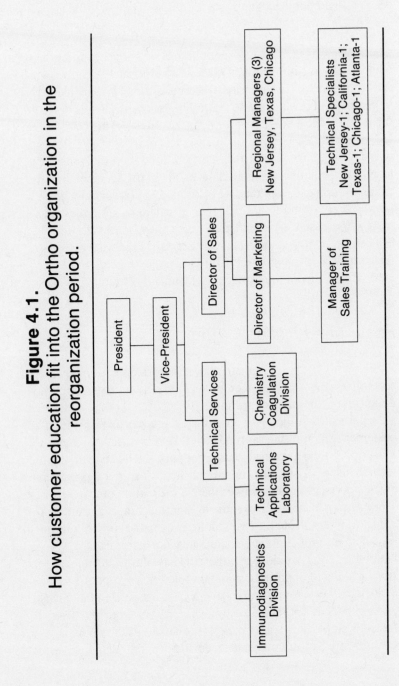

Figure 4.1.
How customer education fit into the Ortho organization in the reorganization period.

President
Vice-President

Technical Services
- Immunodiagnostics Division
- Technical Applications Laboratory
- Chemistry Coagulation Division

Director of Sales
Director of Marketing
- Regional Managers (3) New Jersey, Texas, Chicago
  - Technical Specialists New Jersey-1; California-1; Texas-1; Chicago-1; Atlanta-1
- Manager of Sales Training

tics division of technical services indicated that she was not sure when the transition would be made. She also stated that the decision to disperse the education/technical specialists was made by upper management because it was more cost effective to have them out in the field, closer to their customers. This way, much less time would be spent traveling to customers to teach the free one-day seminars. Under the latest consolidation of centers, the technical specialists would remain at the regional centers. The decision to further consolidate was also made by upper management because, according to the manager of technical resources, there were "too many arms and they were losing central control." Therefore, although the technical specialists reported directly to their regional managers (see figure 4.2), they received all technical assistance from the manager of technical resources.

Postreorganization Period

As of 1980, all the customer training was done by the technical specialists and the manager of technical resources, immunodiagnostics, division of technical services, who showed me a management-by-objectives chart that stated her main function as customer training. She said, however, that in actuality, she spent most of her time answering customer phone calls and helping the technical specialists. She monitored their work but did not have any supervisory authority over them. At the time of this writing, she was responsible for organizing and teaching the case study clinic. She also wrote the case studies used in the course. The purpose of these problems was to simulate what participants see in the laboratory. She would walk the students through problems in small groups of about four persons. The total number of participants would be about twenty. This course was still free of charge to customers and potential customers. Ortho and other Johnson & Johnson employees sometimes would sit in on the course. This was the only connection between customer training and employee training at Ortho. The customers who attended it were selected by the regional managers from a list submitted to them by the sales representatives. In 1980, only one section of the course was offered. In 1981, three were scheduled, one for each region.

Technical specialists conducted seminars and wet workshops as well as two-day mini-case-study clinics throughout the country. They spent about fifty percent of their time out of their offices teaching seminars and workshops. Most of the time workshops were held at hospitals and local hotels. As of 1980, since the tech-

Figure 4.2.
Reporting line for customer education personnel at Ortho Diagnostics, reorganization period.

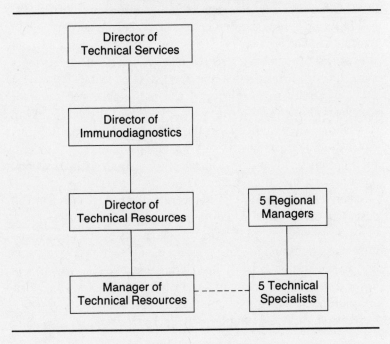

nical specialists had been at the regional centers, they each conducted approximately sixty of the on-site workshops. Prior to 1980, when they were located in New Jersey, each education coordinator would conduct only about fifteen workshops. Part of the reason for such a large differential can be attributed to less travel and part to fewer types of courses offered. Now, all the courses offered are directly related to blood banking. The educational technics course and the Ortho Institute of Laboratory Management are theoretically still on the books, but at present they are not being offered. The manager of technical resources stated: ''Now that the technical specialists are dispersed throughout the country, there is no one to do these programs anymore.''

For all on-site workshops, the sales representatives invited people to attend on a date mutually arrived at with the technical specialist who would be doing the teaching. Often a workshop was established by a sales representative when a customer expressed a need. Other times, a sales representative or a technical specialist would set up a workshop on what they perceived needs to be. A typical class had between twelve and twenty-five students. For on-site workshops, the sales representatives made all the arrangements in regard to location and breaks. The technical specialist provided all the instructional material and samples necessary for the workshop. There were two types of blood banking workshops—wet and dry. In the wet workshops, participants worked on blood samples. This was almost entirely a problem-solving course. The dry workshops were both theoretical and practical, but they did not include working on samples.

When the technical specialists were in the office, they handled customer calls, which could be product or patient related problems. They also assisted sales representatives by answering customer questions and preparing teaching aids. The writing of formal publications and self-instructional packages, which was formerly done by the education coordinators, was now a responsibility of the manager of technical literature, who had been transferred from the Marketing Department to technical services. She either wrote what the sales or marketing departments asked for, or designated someone in technical services to do it. She stated:

> This year we will probably publish only one new book on blood banking. We will probably do one more self-instructional package. Over the long-term we would like to do more, but we're short on help. We are now starting to deal with outside writers, and that should make it easier. I still am publishing ''Reference Points'' and ''Blood Lines'' and material to go along with our products.

With the reorganization, the case-in-point series, a case study approach to continuing education, took on a new face. A $35 charge was initiated for each set of cases. The sets were published once every two months. For this fee, the customer received samples of patient cells and serum and was asked to resolve whatever problems they found. A separate package with the answers or acceptable levels of resolution, discussions, and references was included. Upon completion of each case, customers could apply and receive continuing education units from the American Society of Medical Technology. This new series, released in January 1981, was so successful that by April of 1981 plans were being finalized to produce one each month. A tangential concern was the availability of staff members to monitor the technical accuracy of each case.

The only education function at Ortho that was formally evaluated was the case study clinic. This workshop was evaluated by the participants. They completed an evaluation form at the close of the program. All the persons interviewed expressed the sentiment that if the workshops were not beneficial, they would be difficult to fill. Instead, each workshop was almost always filled to capacity.

In summary, customer education seems to be important at Ortho as part of its customer service program. When the company reorganized, the workshops directly related to Ortho products were the ones that survived. The others were put on the back burner, since Ortho's primary reason for offering customer education was to promote sales. Representatives of the company indicated that a cost-benefit analysis of customer education would be almost impossible. The company considered its customer education program necessary to its reputation as an excellent provider of service. However, Ortho seemed unsure of the most effective way to provide a high quality, cost-effective customer education program.

5
Digital Equipment Corporation

Digital Equipment Corporation designs, manufactures, sells, and services computers and associated peripheral equipment and related software and supplies. At the time of this study, Digital was the largest manufacturer of minicomputers in the world. The company's products are used worldwide in a variety of applications that include scientific research, computation, communications, education, data analysis, industrial control, timesharing, commercial data processing, graphic arts, word processing, health care, instrumentation, engineering, and simulation. In 1978 there were more than ninety thousand Digital computer systems in operation worldwide.

Digital was founded in 1957 by Kenneth Olsen, Stanley Olsen, and Harland Anderson. At the time, they rented eighty-five hundred square feet of space in a woolen mill at Maynard, Massachusetts. Digital now owns the entire mill and many other facilities worldwide. The three men, who were working at the M.I.T. laboratories when they started the company, were 70 percent financed by the American Research and Development Corporation. They started by manufacturing a single product—logic modules.

In fiscal 1980, Digital's total operating revenues exceeded $2 billion and their employees numbered more than fifty-five hundred. Digital has doubled its size every three years since the company began, in both number of employees and total operating revenues. At the close of fiscal 1980, almost twenty thousand people were involved in customer support activities in more than four hundred locations in thirty-seven countries. This included four-teen thousand people engaged in customer service, more than one thousand of whom were professional people involved in full-time customer education. These people are located in the educational services department. According to the company's 1980 annual re-port, Digital's customer orientation is shown by the number of people employed to service customers and is announced as well in the following statement:

> Growth is not our primary goal. Our goal is to be a quality organiza-tion and do a quality job, which means that we will be proud of our work and our products for years to come. As we achieve quality, growth comes as a result. The product we are selling includes the en-gineering, the software, the manufacturing and the services.

Educational Services

The educational services department is responsible for both em-ployee and customer training at Digital. However, the bulk of their work is customer training. The purpose of customer training is to provide specific skills and/or system knowledge to meet indi-vidual customer operational and self-sufficiency needs in order to effectively use a Digital computer system. The department cites two mottos in every issue of *DIGEST:* ''Training when it's needed where it's needed'' and ''Educational Services—Active Partners for Successful Training.'' According to the marketing manager, educational services, eastern division, Digital realizes that train-ing is necessary in order to use a computer; thus, Digital must of-fer it. Without training, customers would not be able to operate Digital systems effectively or efficiently. This would create a neg-ative opinion toward the system, which in turn would create bad publicity for the system and the company. The marketing manager added that Digital has such a large and elaborate customer training program because its upper management believes that their customers' future success depends on their education and training. He further added that "educational services delivered more than 2.7 million student hours of instruction in fiscal 1980 just for customer training. This is equal to a university with six thousand full-time students." The instruction was delivered by five hundred fifty full-time instructors who taught more than three hundred different courses in seventeen languages to more than fifty thousand customer personnel. Their resources included over five hundred computer systems to provide hands-on learning for students. Additionally, Digital's retail computer stores provide customer training designed to introduce operators of small businesses to the use of small computers and word processing systems. These numbers do not include the training Digital offers through individualized self-paced courses.

In addition to these functions, educational services also writes and sells textbooks for academic and industrial users, in both hardware and software technology. They also provide customers with free full-service training consultations to help them determine current and future training needs and to implement cost-effective training programs. Educational services is also responsible for the minicomputer technology program, which trains students for careers in computer service technology. This program is conducted in conjunction with colleges and technical institutes nationwide.

Employee education is part of educational services. Many courses are offered by Digital for their employees, but I was not allowed to see the employee training bulletin because it is confidential. Sometimes employees attend customer education classes, but customers cannot attend employee classes because some information given in those classes is confidential. When interviewed, the marketing manager stated:

> Our employee education course schedule is treated as company confidential for many reasons. Some of the more significant ones include: proprietary information and courses not made available to customers, courses on products and services not yet announced to the public, and different pricing structures for customers and employees.

Digital encourages their employees to take courses at Digital or outside the company. Some training, mostly at the management level, is organized by educational services and held at Digital facilities, but taught by outside people. Sales training is the only training at Digital not conducted by educational services. It is done by the sales department. According to the vice-president of United States sales, this is because effective sales is a constantly evolving and changing process. The only people who can keep up with the process are the people directly involved with sales.

How educational services fits into the Digital organization is shown in figure 5.1. Educational services falls under customer service, which is the responsibility of sales. Thus, the ultimate responsibility for customer training lies with the sales vice-president. He indicated that the sales force uses educational services as a selling tool. According to the marketing manager, Digital's competitors may offer as many courses as Digital but they do not sponsor courses in as many locations. This saves travel time and money for the customer. Both respondents implied that there is a harmonious relationship between educational services and sales, and there does not seem to be any conflict or competition between the two departments.

Educational services has a rather complex internal organization. Everyone involved in customer training eventually reports to the corporate manager of educational services. The department is divided into three divisions—General International Area (Mexico, Canada, and Asia), Europe, and the United States. The United States division is divided into two groups—the western area and the eastern area. The western area consists of training centers in Los Angeles, San Diego, and Dallas. The eastern area comprises training centers in Chicago, Bedford, Massachusetts, New York City, and Washington, D.C. (see figure 5.2). Within the corporate, eastern, and western area structures there are various managers for the different administrative functions, such as marketing and personnel. Each training center has a manager and one to eight supervisors. The training center manager is responsible for planning, organizing, staffing, directing, and controlling the educational services center and staff. The number of instructors in each center varies. For instance, there are twelve instructors in New York and sixteen in Washington. Persons involved in course development and similar support functions are based at corporate headquarters in Massachusetts.

The courses are described and the schedule, including dates and tuition fees, is provided in a newsletter entitled ''DIGEST-Training Update and Schedules,'' published on a quarterly basis. In addition, status reports on training centers, developments in educational technology, and new publications from Digital Press ap-

Figure 5.1.
Educational services in the Digital hierarchy.

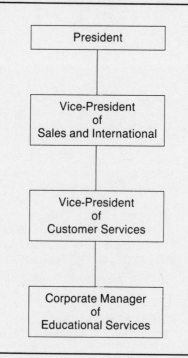

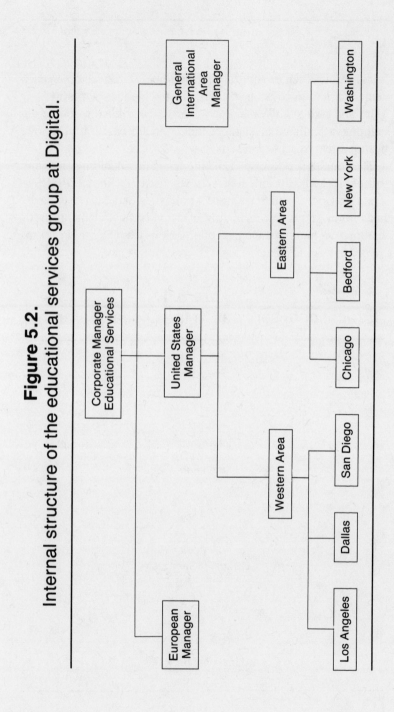

Figure 5.2.

Internal structure of the educational services group at Digital.

pear in "DIGEST." A complete *Customer Training Catalog* is published yearly and categorizes courses as "General Interest," "Languages," "Software," and "Hardware." In addition, separate brochures on the various courses are published. Each brochure is self-contained, giving a total curricula overview and complete course descriptions. The brochure is designed as a planning tool, listing optional formats for each course in the curriculum. Tuition information for each course includes the number of applicable training credits as well as the course price. Also included is information on planning cost-effective training.

Twenty-five customer training centers exist worldwide. Aside from the ones in the United States already mentioned, training centers are located in the following Canadian cities: Vancouver, Edmonton, Calgary, Winnipeg, Toronto, Ottowa, and Halifax. In Europe, there are centers in Paris/Rungis, France; Milan, Italy; Zurich/Oerlikon, Switzerland; London/Reading, United Kingdom; Stockholm/Solna, Sweden; Utrecht, The Netherlands; Madrid, Spain; and Munich, West Germany. The other training centers are in Mexico City, Mexico; Tokyo, Japan; and Sydney, Australia.

Most of Digital's training facilities consist of modern classrooms, a well-equipped computer laboratory, a self-paced learning laboratory, and an audiovisual learning center to support facility courses. In addition, there usually is a student lounge and office space for instructors, the supervisor and/or manager, and a registrar. Digital's largest training center is the corporate training center in Bedford, Massachusetts. It has nearly a quarter-million square feet of space. This facility has seventy-five classrooms, audiovisual learning labs, and more than three hundred terminals available for students and instructors. In fiscal 1979, more than ten thousand students attended classes taught by more than one hundred instructors at this facility.

By comparison, there were eighteen hundred students at the New York City facility and thirty-five hundred at the Washington, D.C., facility during the same time period. Classes at Digital educational centers are normally conducted between 9:00 A.M. and

5:00 P.M. Monday through Friday. However, laboratory sessions may be conducted in the evening to ensure ample time working on the computer.

The marketing manager indicated that all instructors are recruited from academia rather than private industry because Digital wants to hire experienced teachers. Instructors are full-time employees at Digital. All instructors take training courses at corporate headquarters in Bedford on how to operate the various systems. Most of the other professional people in educational services are involved behind the scene, primarily in course development. Their major functions include: course development; production of outlines, graphs, and audiovisual materials; translating material into foreign languages; and monitoring quality.

Digital's courses range from introductory to advanced. The types of programs available cover three areas. The Selective Seminar Program provides conceptual training for secretaries, managers, programmers, and analysts. Four seminars are offered in this program—two are three days long and two are two days. Digital also offers a complete course curriculum on both hardware and on software. Hardware courses are a series of maintenance training programs that have been designed for the customer who is planning to do some level of self-maintenance on this computer system. Software courses are designed to educate the customer in the operation, program development, and management of software systems. Forty-six different hardware courses are offered and an additional eighty software courses, all for varying lengths of time.

In 1980, Digital offered a series of seminars entitled "A New Direction for the 80s." Each of these seminars included case studies, small group discussions, and lectures designed to facilitate a practical understanding and a comprehensive review of each topic. These seminars were aimed at the nontechnical user.

Two formats exist for Digital's training programs—lecture/laboratory courses and self-paced instruction courses. Both types of courses can be held either at the customer's location or at one of Digital's training centers in North America. By 1979, between 20

Table 5.1.
Hardware and software courses by course length.

Hardware Courses		Software Courses	
Length	Number	Length	Number
2 Days	1	2 Days	1
3 Days	3	3 Days	9
4 Days	1	5 Days	56
5 Days	23	10 Days	7
10 Days	13	Varying	7
15 Days	5		

and 30 percent of all Digital's educational activities were rendered at the customer's location. Some courses are also given at the training centers outside the United States.

Some courses are specially tailored to the customer's needs; these are usually held at the customer's site. They offer the advantages of greater time flexibility and a savings in travel and living expenses over the courses held at the training centers. These on-site courses deal only with the topics needed, so the length of the courses can be shortened, and they can offer greater in-depth training since they have to deal only with an individual application. Typically, they comprise a series of courses and can be modified from existing courses or developed as an entirely new program from mutually agreed upon educational objectives. All standard courses are available as ''Exclusives-at-Digital-Facility.'' This training option not only allows employees to cover specific job-related situations, but also allows for confidentiality if a customer needs to discuss proprietary information. Most standard courses have between two and twenty students with ten as the average number of students per class. However, Digital has run classes as large as one hundred fifty and as small as one.

Lecture/Laboratory Courses

Lecture/laboratory courses are a form of group learning. The elements of this format include printed course materials and manuals, oral presentations and supporting graphic displays, written and laboratory exercises, periodic testing, evaluative feedback to learners, and interaction with an instructor who is a subject matter specialist. Aside from the benefit of interaction with an experienced instructor, this type of course offers interaction with other students. The instructor provides help for individual learning problems and assistance with specialized applications. Most courses include intensive hands-on computer exercises, and all use a broad collection of reference manuals and instructional materials. The course material distributed is included in the fee and is designed to support course content. However, the material does not necessarily include all technical references for the product.

At present, Digital has a group of people working on what they call the Dover project. The purpose of the project is to get their lecture/laboratory courses accredited by four-year Massachusetts colleges. Some courses have already been accredited, but I could not determine how many or which ones.

Self-Paced Instruction

Self-paced instruction (SPI) courses, a form of individualized learning, were established to help meet the need for a more economical training method than the traditional lecture/laboratory format. Maintaining training centers is expensive. SPI courses have the advantage of being expedient and much less expensive. The elements of the SPI format may include printed materials, audiovisual presentations, computer assisted instruction, or some mix of the three. SPI courses are completely self-contained. They are divided into modular instructional units, exercises, and tests. This permits the student to enter any one of several levels and to select only those specific topics, or more specialized areas, which meet their job requirements.

SPI courses may be taken at an individualized learning center at one of the Digital education centers, where the student has available to him audiovisual equipment, a computer, a study carrel, and subject matter experts. These courses may also be taken at the job site, but in order to ensure the training success of this individualized program, a subject matter professional who can properly manage and support the course must be provided. Digital recommends that the courses administrator enroll in a Digital facility version of the course prior to administering the SPI course at his or her own facility. This ensures that the administrator is familiar with the methods and objectives of the course. Access to a computer for lab exercises may also be required. When the proper conditions do exist, the student will achieve the benefits of the SPI format: studying at his or her own pace, taking only those lessons needed, scheduling study hours to suit individual needs, and realizing the economies that on-site training makes possible. However, the SPI form is recommended only for the experienced student. When used at the job site, SPI aids customers by providing high quality training at any time to their employees while having them readily available if needed. Additionally, travel and living expenses are not incurred. Aside from achieving economies in delivery, SPI courses are more consistent than lecture/laboratory courses since the idiosyncracies of instructors do not exist. Also, once purchased, the SPI course can be reused for future training needs, including upgrading of employees, retraining, and remaining as a reference source.

SPI courses are packaged in binders and provide manuals and printed course materials (including graphics), printed practice exercises and solutions, instructions for hands-on exercises, and tests (supplied with correct answers) for self-evaluation. If the package is audiovisual, it consists of workbooks for ten students, study guides, reference books, a choice of videocassettes with workbooks, sixteen millimeter filmstrip/audio cartridges with workbooks or audio tapes with workbooks, and additional source material. SPI courses include a manager's kit that contains instructions for properly administering the course, course goals, a course map through the material, and prerequisites for the course. The workbooks supplement the concepts studied in the modules with additional reading and reinforce them with exercises that provide the feedback necessary to the learning process. Students alternate between using the audiovisual programs and the workbook, which results in a program consisting of listening, viewing, reading, and writing. This integrated approach adds variety to learning and can help to keep up the student's interest. The tests are designed to allow the student, or the course administrator, to judge the student's degree of mastery and to slow down or speed up the training accordingly.

I spoke to a group of students who were taking a self-paced course while they were sitting in a lounge area outside one of the individualized learning centers at the New York training center. According to these students, Digital includes a lounge area and eating area with vending machines at each training center, so there is a place for students to go when they need a study break. The New York training center manager said they would rather have a student rest on a couch or lounge chair than look half asleep at a study carrel.

One of the students indicated that he preferred taking self-paced courses at a Digital facility because the environment was more conducive to concentrating on the material than at his place of employment, and there was no one around to interrupt him. He found he was able to get through the material faster. Another student added that the course administrator at Digital was much more knowledgeable and helpful than persons at his own company. The three students all agreed that they found the self-paced and audiovisual courses more useful than the lecture/laboratory courses they had previously taken. They especially enjoyed the freedom to work at their own pace and the instant feedback they received when taking tests on the computer. They found this type of independent learning to be more motivating.

Audio-Visual Courses

Audiovisual training at Digital began in 1974. The audiovisual instruction that educational services developed, as part of their self-paced instructional packages, is available in several formats:

1. Sixteen millimeter filmstrip/audio cartridges with workbooks;
2. videocassettes with workbooks;
3. visual flipbooks with audiotape and workbooks;
4. audiotapes with workbooks only.

These courses vary in size from a course with a two hundred page workbook and accompanying audiotape to a course with thirty-six filmstrip/audio cartridges, four thousand visuals, and fifteen hundred pages of text. According to the manager of instructional media design and development, these courses are developed using the format shown in figure 5.3.

The process indicated in figure 5.3 is conducted by a team consisting of instructional media designers, audiovisual course developers, hardware and software consultants, and numerous publishing and printing production personnel, such as artists and editors. Only courses that educational services feels are effective for audiovisual instruction are selected to be packaged in this format. All audiovisual courses contain tests that have been designed to allow either the administrator or the student to judge quickly the degree of student mastery and to slow down or speed up the training accordingly.

Audiovisual courses offer many benefits to the students as well as their employers. These courses allow students to progress at their own rate, to train at their own and the company's convenience, to directly apply their knowledge to the company's particular application while they are learning, and to study only the modules most pertinent to their job needs. They also eliminate the cost to the company of a formal classroom instructor and of travel and lodging.

Computer-Based Education

Computer-based education courses are those that use the computer itself as the medium for delivering instruction. This includes computer-assisted testing (CAT), computer-managed instruction (CMI), and computer-assisted instruction (CAI). Computer-assisted testing occurs when the computer grades tests on material studied in the self-paced or lecture mode, shares student data, and generates reports on student and class statuses. Computer-

Figure 5.3.
Digital audiovisual course development sequence.

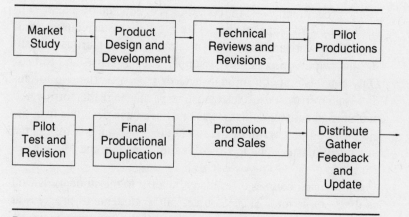

managed instruction occurs when the computer administers as well as grades tests on material studied off-line, stores student data, and prescribes learning materials based on a student's performance record. Computer-assisted instruction occurs when the computer presents on-line instruction to students in an interactive mode in addition to performing the functions of computer-assisted testing and computer-managed instruction.

In May 1983, Digital announced IVIS (Interactive Video Information System), the next step in their computer-based education efforts. This system combines Digital's micro/professional computer with videodisc so that the self-paced instructions include interactive computer graphics, high quality color video, and high fidelity audio. The system mixes-and-matches this to produce computer-aided courseware with video.

An example of a computer-based education course is one entitled the "Basic Primer." This is a self-paced, computer-managed course consisting of four interlocking pieces: core material, extended material, CMI system software, and a course administrator's guide. It is intended to teach the fundamentals of BASIC language programming to people who have no previous experience with computers.

The core material consists of the first seven modules in the course, which are bound into a single book. Each of the modules has a corresponding test that is part of the CMI system software. The extended material, which consists of eight modules, is in a second book. These materials are more advanced, and all students taking the course are not expected to complete them. Like the core material, each module has a corresponding on-line test. The CMI system software maintains a class roster that shows the status of all students, administers and scores pretests and posttests for each module in the course, and directs students through the course by routing them from one module to the next and by identifying areas in which they need further study. The course administrator's guide is written for an experienced system manager and indicates how to install the CMI system software on the customer's own computer system and how to build the required data base. It also gives a detailed description of how to run the program that is used by system managers to initialize the data base and monitor the progress of all students in the course.

Students work through the BASIC primer by studying modules off-line and taking tests on-line. This is done according to the scheme in the flowchart shown in figure 5.4. An example of what a CMI package looks like is in Appendix B.

According to the manager of computer-based course development, computer-based courses at Digital are developed by a team consisting of three types of experts and coordinated by a project manager. The subject matter expert fully understands the material and ensures that the course content is technically correct. He or she concentrates on what should be taught. The instructional media specialist ensures that the computer medium is used appropriately and creatively and that the material is instructionally valid. He or she works with the subject matter expert to plan the entire program and the types of interactions students will have with the computer system. In other words, the media specialist decides on the most effective way to present the material. The third type of expertise needed for the development of computer-based materials is provided by a computer programmer. He concentrates on how the computer will teach or how to implement the material determined by the subject matter expert. The project manager's responsibility is to set priorities and determine which strategies the group can afford to implement.

Cost

Educational services is a profit-making division at Digital. In figuring their profit, educational services considers all expenses, including personnel, facilities, capital equipment, depreciation and amortization, utilities, material, and travel. Thus, the fees charged directly or indirectly (included in the price of the product) for training, cover all the department's expenses.

The prices for Digital's training programs vary. In general, in 1980, standard on-site courses cost $4,400 per course week for software courses and $5,000 per course week for hardware courses plus travel and expenses. Exclusive-at-facility courses also cost $5,000 per course week. Custom courses are priced at

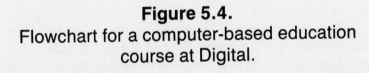

Figure 5.4.
Flowchart for a computer-based education course at Digital.

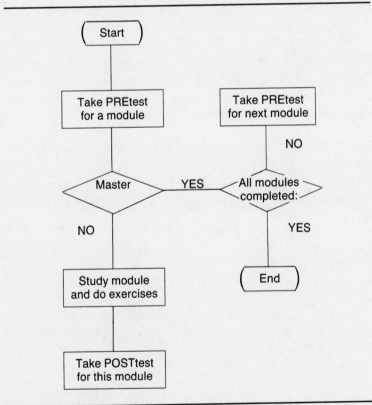

the same rate as on-site courses, plus an additional course development charge that is directly related to preparation and development time. These prices include training for up to ten students for five days; the charge for each additional student is $200. The price includes all training materials, the instructor's travel in North America, and the instructor's fee per diem. The prices for the standard courses offered at Digital education centers are shown in table 5.2.

Self-paced instruction (SPI) courses that do not include an audiovisual component are priced from $30 for a course with one sixty page binder to $1,495 for a course containing one computer-managed instruction, system software, one administrator's guide (fifty pages), and ten sets of core course materials (a 470 page book). Quantity discounts are available for SPI courses. The costs for SPI courses which contain audiovisual materials are somewhat higher. Courses on videocassette range from $2,000 to $5,000. Courses on audio-filmstrip cartridges cost $300 to $700 less than their videocassette equivalent.

Table 5.2
Cost of course by course length.

Course Length	Course Price Per Student
2 Days	$ 255
2½ Days	$ 395
3 Days	$ 345—$ 450
4 Days	$ 600
5 Days	$ 345—$ 650
10 Days	$ 950—$1,300
15 Days	$1,800
30 Days	$4,500

When customers purchase a Digital software system, they are issued "training credits," the number depending upon the system purchased. These training credits allow the customer to obtain free training in programming techniques, system operation, and applications. One training credit can be applied for one week of instruction for one student at any of the general interest, language, or software courses conducted by educational services. Training credits cannot be applied toward payment for attending hardware courses, purchased SPI and audiovisual courses, or Digital Press publications. Courses lasting less than one week are also available at one training credit per student. Training credits may be used for audiovisual courses taken at one of the individualized learning centers. Ten training credits may redeem a standard software on-site program, excluding the cost of the instructor's travel. Training credits are valid for one year from their date of issue, and may not be retroactively applied toward courses that have been previously taken.

The number of training credits issued for a particular system is determined by the group at Digital responsible for manufacturing the system in conjunction with educational services. They try to determine the amount of training that is needed for a person with an appropriate background to effectively and efficiently use the system. Usually, educational services presents a training proposal to the product line people. They, in turn, trim back or expand the training. Then there is some negotiation between the two groups until a decision is made on how much training is needed and how many training credits must be issued to cover it. The cost of providing this training is built into the price of the system. Training credits are usually enough to cover the training of only one person. They are meant to get customers started on their new system.

To determine what types of training (methods) are the most convenient and cost effective, Digital suggests that the customer examine, in detail, the features and benefits of the various training formats—lecture/laboratory, audiovisual and self-paced instruction without audiovisual. For example, table 5.3 evaluates the alternative training methods and costs for the course "Introduction to Minicomputers."

Table 5.3

Alternative training methods and cost for "Introduction to Minicomputers"

ALTERNATIVES	Current Costs (2 Students)		Future Costs (1 Student)		Total Costs (3 Students)	
	Including Travel	Tuition Only	Including Travel	Tuition Only	Including Travel	Tuition Only
Lecture/Lab Courses						
$450/Student Tuition	$ 900	$ 900	$ 450	$ 450	$1350	$1350
$550/Student Travel	1100		550		1650	
Total	$2000	$ 900	$1000	$ 450	$3000	$1350
Audiovisual at Training Center						
$345/Student Tuition	$ 690	$ 690	$ 345	$ 345	$1035	$1035
$550/Student Travel	1100		550		1650	
Total	$1790	$ 690	$ 895	$ 345	$2685	$1035
Usage of purchased						
Audiovisual material at job-site	$1950	$1950	$ 0	$ 0	$1950	$1950
Playback Unit/Audiovisual Equipment	499		0	0	499	
Total	$2449	$1950	$ 0	$ 0	$2449	$1950

Reprinted by permission of Digital Equipment Corporation.

Identifying Training Needs

Educational services identifies current and future training needs by manpower analysis and skill analysis. For manpower analysis, they consider the training needs for at least two years, including retraining, for each job classification. For knowledge and skill analysis, Digital has constructed flowcharts that show the exact courses required for thorough training in each job classification to operate a particular system effectively. In addition, the flowchart specifies the exact sequence in which courses should be taken and how long each lasts. Digital emphatically suggests that adequate on-the-job time be allowed between courses so that skills may be perfected and mastered. The knowledge and skills of current staff members must be analyzed and the job requirements for future staff must be defined in order to determine the level and number of courses needed for each person in each job classification.

The $550 a week travel allowance includes transportation and accommodation expenses. The figures used do not include the benefit of equipment depreciation, if purchased, or possible tuition increases. Based on these figures, Digital recommends using audiovisual courses at their individualized learning centers because the costs are lower than the charges for lecture/laboratory courses. This format was chosen over the outright purchase of the program plus playback equipment because the number of people needing training is small and it was assumed that the sample company does not have qualified supervisory personnel for the course. If these conditions change, then purchasing the audiovisual program may become the better option. This type of analysis is done for each course needed.

Course Development

Before a new course is offered, the educational services marketing department conducts a market survey. This is usually a simple process. If a need is perceived, a group of course developers will outline a course. Then, customers are asked if they would be interested in such a course. Sometimes this is done by a direct letter to the customers, but more often by an announcement in *Digest*. For example, on page four of the January-June 1980 *Digest,* a headline reads, "Logistics Management Course Planned." An explanation is given for the course that includes the major topics to be covered. There is also an inquiry form which states, "Yes, we are interested in your new Logistics Management Seminar." The form also asks for basic information like name, title, company, and address. It also asks the customer to state the number of persons who wish to attend and the preferred location. In this particular case, the response was poor so the course was never offered. This procedure is not followed for operator, user, and assembly line courses since these courses are directly related to a particular system and are necessary in order to operate the system.

Digital has three course development groups—one for the lecture/laboratory courses, one for the computer administered courses, and one for the audiovisual instruction. Digital uses the systematic instructional design model described in figure 5.5 for their course development process. They conduct a study of customer jobs, tailor instruction to those jobs, and then rely on corrective feedback to ensure that the instruction is both effective and instrumental in helping educational services to reach its ultimate goal of preparing customers to efficiently use a Digital computer.

An educational technologist at Digital gave the following detailed description of the model used by Digital. He indicated that the primary purpose of a task description is to identify the on-the-job skills a customer needs. It identifies what is required for one to be competent at a particular job. The description is derived from the observations of job holders, from questionnaires, or from interviews. The primary purpose of a task analysis is to obtain task description results for the types of skills involved, such as recalling facts, defining concepts, and solving problems. Sequencing and grouping are necessary because some skills have to be learned before others either because they are prerequisites or because a certain sequence will make learning easier. The skills to be learned in each lesson unit are then summarized in the statement of objectives.

Statements of objectives serve a dual purpose. They assist the course developer in keeping to relevant goals, and the learner uses them to gear his efforts to the material. Objectives also serve as the starting point for test construction. Tests reveal which job-relevant skills have been effectively learned. Test results also identify which sections of course material do or do not work and identify for students which objectives they have or have not accomplished. Tests, then, are a source of evaluative feedback.

A primary goal in formulating an instructional strategy is to design learning experiences capable of accommodating distinctive subject matter and target audience requirements, because different types of skills call for different teaching approaches and learners often differ widely in ability, training, or experience. Instructional strategies are translated into actual training materials and procedures. In Digital's lecture/laboratory format, lecture materials, transparencies, manuals, and student handouts are packaged together. In the self-paced format, all training materials are self-contained. There is an actual layout of course materials and procedures to identify what works and what does not work. Changes are then made accordingly. Test results, questionnaire results, and informal conversations between the students and the instructors are the basis for revisions. For example, in 1979, Digital established a self-paced computer language course that was field tested at three educational institutions in New England.

Evaluation

Digital has an extensive evaluation program with constant feedback on long-term trends and short-term problems. For the past ten years, Digital has sent out a ''Comprehensive Customer Satisfaction Survey'' to all customers with hardware service contracts. Recently, the survey was expanded to include software services

Figure 5.5.
Digital's approach to the systematic design of instruction.

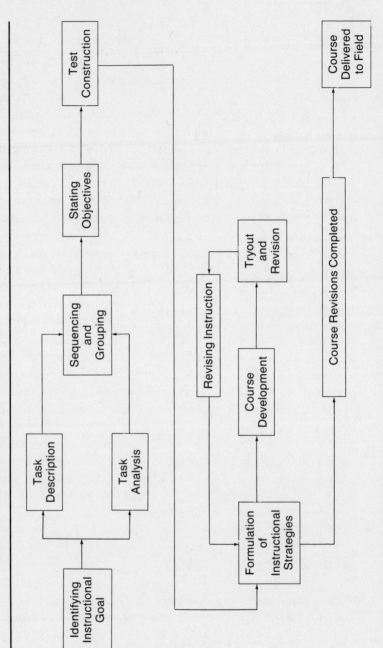

customers. The survey deals with the three main areas of customer services—field services, software services, and educational services.

Digital's courses are specifically evaluated through their quality assurance (QA) program. The purpose of this program is to objectively demonstrate that the quality of training can be assessed. The major goals of the QA program are to ensure that students actually acquire job-related knowledge and skills and to reinforce the consistency and uniformity of all the courses offered. Thus, no matter where a course is taught, students will achieve predefined objectives and use standardized tests. The tests, which are individualized, are used to assess the level of the student. This allows each student to receive the maximum from each course according to his individual ability. Educational services emphasizes that learning can be assured only if the student is able to meet the prerequisites for each course and that it is the customer's responsibility to ensure this.

In the QA program students test themselves prior to each course to ensure that they have the needed prerequisite knowledge. Tests, which are taken at various points in each course, consist of multiple choice questions. Questionnaires are also filled out by instructors as they observe students perform the steps in a given procedure. All tests are designed to be machine scored, so the student can receive performance reports right away. This continuous feedback process allows students to track their own progress. The system also allows the instructors and administrators to monitor the overall progress of students so they may provide assistance where and when it is needed.

The QA program also utilizes a student opinion form (see Appendix C) to systematically assess student suggestions and comments. This form has been field-tested and statistically adjusted to ensure that it acts as an accurate reporting instrument. Instructors express their opinions about the course on an instructor opinion form. Both these forms record impressions of course effectiveness, of the materials and environment, and of the degree to which the course fulfilled expectations. Results from both forms are kept on file with the other course data. According to the field service training representative, a new student opinion form is presently being field-tested for the self-paced courses so a more accurate assessment of this type of course may be made.

Both forms are analyzed on a local basis. Every Digital training center has a computer system that scores, tallies, and summarizes the input from these opinion forms. Detailed reports are printed for students and instructors. The system also produces reports that analyze and evaluate the overall quality of each course in summary form, since individual student reports are kept confidential. These summary reports are produced by corporate educational services in Bedford, Massachusetts.

Retail Stores

Digital opened its first retail stores in 1978. A Digital retail store is a place where owners of small businesses can go to learn how a computer can help them in a cost-effective manner. The objective of these stores is to sell small systems with standard software to businesses that require such products. They have "get acquainted" slide shows as well as seminars. This is the only setting where educational services uses training as a selling tool. The retail stores are located in major metropolitan areas nationwide. The stores were started because it is not economical for a salesperson to do extensive traveling to try to sell a small, relatively inexpensive computer system or word processor.

The initial "training" consists of an open, free seminar called "Benefits of Small Computer Systems," which lasts for about one hour and discusses the advantages of owning a small business computer system in terms of efficiency and profitability. The instructor frequently uses customer testimonials to illustrate his points. A slide presentation also aids his talk. This workshop is usually presented on a weekly basis.

Another workshop is entitled "Information Processing Systems for Small Businesses—An Introduction." This seminar, for which a nominal fee is charged, describes the concepts and techniques behind low-cost business computing systems and how they can be used to improve business performance. Topics covered include hardware and software system components, application packages, and basic systems analysis. The instructor walks the class through a typical business application. The course is designed to demystify the computer and give participants a basic understanding of what a computer is, how it works, and introduce some of the basic vocabulary.

A third course offered by retail stores is "Case Studies," a lecture workshop that provides an in-depth treatment of the customer applications presented in the introductory workshop: payroll, general ledger, accounts payable and receivable, billing, inventory control, and sales analysis. This is a highly interactive session with lots of discussion and direct application to each participant's business. The instructor/salesperson also discusses rudimentary analytical tools needed for assessing a company's computer requirements. A nominal fee is charged for this seminar.

The fourth workshop is entitled "System Design Concepts for the Small Business." This workshop describes the basic concepts of the "system analysis" approach and how this approach can be used to design office systems involving new computers. Participants are asked to analyze a portion of their own business and determine what changes in their business operation might be necessary to obtain the maximum benefit from a new business system. This is reviewed with the entire class.

The final offering at Digital retail stores is on "Word Processing." This is a lecture and hands-on demonstration session for those persons unfamiliar with word processing in a business environment. It reviews the basic terminology and fundamental skills needed to use a Digital word processing system.

All workshops are taught by salespeople. In this respect, this before-the-sale training comes under the umbrella of the sales department. However, educational services writes all the materials and prepares all the audiovisual presentations for these instructors. This is the only time Digital utilizes training for the sole purpose of increasing sales. The workshops are not evaluated from an educational standpoint. Their success is measured by the number of sales that result from the sessions.

Minicomputer Technology Program

The minicomputer technology program (MTP) is a cooperative venture between Digital and various colleges and technical institutes. This program is operated through the educational services organization. The purpose of the program is to train people for careers in computer services technology (CST). Most schools do not have such a program, although they may offer a computer science curriculum. For this program the colleges provide the teaching expertise and facilities. Digital provides the necessary equipment and learning materials. The desired result of this synergism is to help colleges implement up-to-date, cost-effective, two-year curricula that will provide industry, particularly Digital, with people who have entry-level skills in computer service technology.

Digital will sell the equipment to a school at a nominal cost. In the beginning, they gave the equipment away, but this policy was discontinued because the schools tended to use the computers for their own administrative work rather than for its intended purpose. When a school has to pay for the equipment, even if only a nominal amount, they need to justify the expense and, therefore, are more likely to use it for its intended purpose.

Although instructors are employed by the school, Digital trains them to teach in the MTP program. Digital recommends that MTP faculty take the same courses that Digital's regular customers take. The major areas of study for MTP faculty include introductory self-paced audiovisual courses (generic and product related), introductory software, advanced software, processor and options maintenance, and peripheral maintenance. Digital also recommends that MTP faculty participate in summer internships with

Digital's local field service groups. The internships are especially useful to those responsible for curriculum planning and development. Digital provides MTP faculty with documentation for use in the classroom and the computer lab, any available instructor guides, lab guides, and reference documentation related to the CST curriculum.

Digital also provides the schools with the same audiovisual courses that its field service organization uses for its training program. These are used as supplements to lectures and as remedial work. Digital also allows students to obtain on-the-job training so they will be able to measure their ability to work under pressure, to accept responsibility, to perform efficiently while meeting deadlines, and to gain exposure to customer relations. Digital benefits from this arrangement by seeing how each student functions. The company usually hires the persons they are satisfied with. Digital benefits by acquiring new technicians whose training is tax deductible to the company.

Digital employs regional coordinators to identify schools for the MTP program on the basis of recommendations made by the field service managers and other MTP staff members. According to one regional field service training representative, when a school in his area indicates an interest in the program, he arranges a meeting between MTP staff members and school representatives. The purpose of the first meeting is to introduce the MTP program and to determine the school's potential for involvement. If the school decides to establish a MTP program, follow-up meetings are held to make curriculum recommendations and to determine the extent of the support the college will receive. Most institutions involved in this program are two-year colleges or technical institutes. Two years of training is all that is usually needed for someone to become a computer service technologist. Again, Digital's primary purpose for conducting this program is to train CSTs, many of whom will become employed by Digital. A secondary purpose for conducting the program is for students to get used to seeing and operating Digital equipment. The principle here is that if the students become familiar with the equipment they will prefer it to a competitor's product. This is ''future'' customer training.

Before a school enters the MTP program, Digital and the college must agree on curriculum objectives and content. When these are established, recommendations are made based on skill and knowledge requirements for Digital's field service technicians, plus the following considerations:

1. Applicable on-going courses
2. Needs of local employers for CST graduates
3. Faculty loads
4. General educational requirements
5. Local, regional, and professional accreditation
6. College entrance requirement for a CST curriculum

As an MPT participant, the school, which must be nonprofit, is required to assume certain responsibilities to ensure the success of its CST curriculum. This includes meeting specific objectives in a number of areas:

1. Establishing and continuing a quality CST curriculum
2. Providing students and faculty
3. Using the resources Digital provides effectively
4. Ensuring minority and female enrollments

Digital evaluates the MTP program by conducting informal visits by the local MTP staff each term and formal visits by the corporate and field staffs annually. Schools are also encouraged to make recommendations on ways to improve the program. Digital justifies the cost because their services and equipment are a tax-deductible expense. A regional field service training representative said that the biggest problem with this program is meeting all the requests for setting up a program and continuing to provide the necessary support services after the program is instituted.

DECUS

DECUS is a computer users' society for Digital customers. It is the largest and most active computer users' society in the industry, with thirty-six thousand members. DECUS issues papers, supports publications, provides a forum for the exchange of ideas, holds meetings, and makes available a software library containing more than seventeen hundred active programs. Each year DECUS holds a symposium in a different part of the country. Educational services holds a lecture symposium at this time, and they have an exhibit area. The objective of the symposium is to give customers an overview of Digital products and services. The educational services exhibit gives customers the opportunity to participate in computer-based education demonstrations, examine self-paced instruction printed material, and try an audiovisual learning program. Educational services also conduct special question and answer sessions that enable customers to address product-specific training questions.

Summary

The educational services group at Digital Equipment Corporation, which is composed of more than one thousand professional employees, offers many courses in various formats for its customers. The training relates to the use and maintenance of Digital hardware and software systems and provides general information about computers in general. Digital offers individualized and group training at its own training centers and at its customers' locations. The training incorporates various techniques and instructional aids and can include: instruction, lectures, demonstrations, audiovisual presentations, and product literature. According to the corporate manager of educational services, Digital's primary reasons for having such an elaborate customer training program are to teach proper use of Digital products and to promote product awareness and customer satisfaction. Using their quality assurance system, Digital has determined that their customer training is effective in teaching proper use of Digital products and in increasing awareness of those products. Educational services is uncertain whether or not their courses have resulted in increased sales for Digital or whether they help to reduce service and maintenance calls. They do know that the salespeople use the training offered by educational services as a selling tool.

6
Jersey Central Power & Light Company

Jersey Central Power & Light Company (JCP&L) is an electric utility that has a large customer/consumer education program. In chapter 1, a distinction is drawn between customer education and consumer education. JCP&L is an exception to this distinction due to the nature of its product. Electricity is a necessity for most people, but for conservation reasons, its use needs to be curtailed. Additionally, individuals cannot choose who they buy their electricity from. Although JCP&L's program is for its customers only, it does not promote the sale of its product. Therefore, in this case, there is no distinction between consumer and customer education, and the terms can be used interchangeably.

JCP&L has several types of customer education programs. One kind involves informal and one-on-one instruction given by members of the consumer services department. Another consists of group learning activities led by members of the corporate communications department (figure 6.1). In addition JCP&L provides product literature, sent as inserts from time to time with monthly bills and as handouts at meetings or on individual customer requests for assistance. Sample titles include: "Energy Management Ideas for Kilowattchers," "Household Safety Tips," "Tips on Appliance Service," and "Storms—Are you Prepared?" The consumer services department, which sponsors the informal customer education, was formerly the company's sales department. At that time, they promoted increased use of electrical energy. They did this by going to such places as appliance stores and giving cooking demonstrations on an electric range. For this type of program, the manager of a store would get customers to attend the demonstration by giving them a nominal gift. However, since the early 1970's, the Public Utilities Commission has not allowed utility companies to promote increased use of electricity. Instead, under the Residential Conservation Service Program of the National Energy Act, all utilities must promote the other side of the coin—energy conservation. In order to accomplish this task, the consumer services department at JCP&L employs seventeen residential builder representatives who spend approximately 30 percent of their time conducting audits on private homes and informally teaching their customers what they can do to save energy and money, for example, increasing insulation, lowering thermostats, and adding storm windows. According to a home energy savings program assistant at the state department of energy, the auditor's training was done by the utilities and testing was done by the department of energy. This service, which is heavily subsidized by JCP&L, cost $15 per visit per household in 1980 if the household was all electric. If the customer had oil heat, he or she could have a test for oil burner efficiency done by the Fuel Merchants Association. This would carry an additional $10 fee. In 1981, the fee was lowered to $15 for the total package. If the home was all electric, JCP&L would receive $15. If it were an oil and electric home, JCP&L would receive $5 and the Fuel Merchants Association would receive $10. According to the New Jersey department of energy's home energy savings program manager, the fee was determined because the department of energy, through a study conducted by the Eagleton Institute at Rutgers University, determined that most residential customers were not likely to pay more than $15 for an audit. JCP&L estimated that in 1980 it actually cost them $75 per audit.

JCP&L's manager of consumer services said that this type of customer education "has to be informal because we are not selling a finite product." Under the department of energy program, JCP&L sends an announcement of this home energy savings program along with customers' bills. The announcement also in-

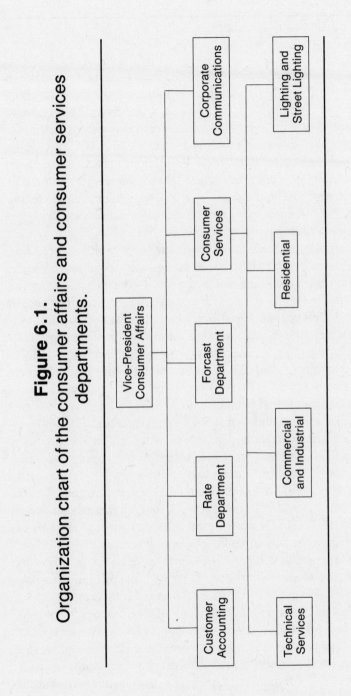

Figure 6.1.

Organization chart of the consumer affairs and consumer services departments.

cludes a list of energy conservation measures and practices. The cost of this service is shared by JCP&L with the local gas utility. The gas company pays for part of the bill insert. The reason for this particular arrangement is that everyone has electricity but not everyone has gas, so this way the information will reach every household with no duplication. In addition, JCP&L, as well as the other utilities, sends on request other materials listed in the announcement. These include a do-it-yourself home energy survey workbook, a guide to residential insulation, a financing guide, and a guide to performing home energy conservation improvements.

The consumer services department also employs fifteen commercial and industrial representatives who spend approximately 25 percent of their time conducting audits for this type of client and making recommendations on energy conservation. The auditors who have been employed by JCP&L for many years all have a sales background because of the former nature of the department. The new auditors can have any background. They receive most of their training in the field. However, their training is supplemented by meetings with speakers who address different topics, such as insulation and solar heating.

The group training that JCP&L conducts is based out of the corporate communications department, which is part of consumer affairs. These efforts are coordinated by the consumer relations manager. At present, there are twenty-eight people involved in this program, four full time and twenty-four part time. The four full-timers include the manager. All four are trained home economists who were formerly in the sales department. The part-time people are part of a speakers bureau. These people are full-time employees who volunteer their time to speak in the area of their expertise to various groups. Their only payment is a thank-you dinner sponsored by JCP&L at the end of each year.

All these programs and the material distributed at the programs are free for JCP&L customers. Speakers will go to schools or to any organization that requests a program. The subject matter discussed by the consumer relations staff is varied. The topics include energy conservation, nuclear energy, and the like. The consumer relations manager said, "The Susie Homemaking thing of promoting electricity is gone forever."

The members of the speakers bureau will discuss almost anything related to their expertise and related to JCP&L's work. For example, if a customer requests a presentation on nuclear generation, a member of the generation department will speak. Other topics include meter tampering, safety, alternate sources of energy, and rates. The speakers bureau was started three years ago. At least once each year a flyer, included as an insert with a monthly bill, describes the program. The flyer says:

> JCP&L has trained qualified speakers who are prepared to speak on energy-related subjects.
>
> Presentations by JCP&L's speakers are designed to meet the needs of each individual program. They are available without charge for adult and school groups. Speakers can be scheduled to participate in any of the following:
>
> - Informal group discussions
> - Sessions with films, slides or visuals, followed by questions and answers
> - Formal prepared speeches
> - Opening remarks, followed by question and answer sessions
> - Panel discussions
> - Radio or television presentations.
>
> Topics include:
>
> - Energy sources, present and future—what can we use?
> - Energy management/conservation—what's in it for you?
> - Energy and the environment—is there a connection?
> - The energy crisis—does it exist?
> - Utility economics—what affects the cost of electricity?
> - Nuclear energy—why is it necessary?
> - Electrical safety—why is it important?
> - Other topics are available upon request.

This group's quota for programs in 1980 was 225 adult programs and 330 youth programs. However, they actually conducted 670 programs reaching 45,519 people. This number does not include the people reached via radio or closed circuit television. In 1980 there were 12 programs on closed circuit television and a half-dozen radio shows. Nor does it include the students reached when a teacher videotapes a presentation to one class and shows the tape to the entire school. In addition to announcing this service in a monthly bill, the corporate communications department sends out letters to the 602 principals in their service area. Included are public, private, and parochial schools. One reason this small group of people is able to accommodate all their requests is that they often do several presentations in one day. The consumer relations manager said that the other reason is that, ''We're dedicated people.'' She added, ''We [the consumer relations staff and the speakers bureau] are the liaison between the company and the customer. Our clientele ranges from kindergarten through senior citizens. We reach a lot of people. We do a more than adequate job with the resources that we have.''

The busiest times of year for programs are fall and spring. For instance, in October 1980, 51 adult programs and 40 youth programs were conducted for 5,734 people and in November, 114 programs were conducted. The summer is slow because schools and many civic groups do not hold meetings at this time of year. A bill insert, which is sent out once a year, describes the speakers bureau. The consumer relations staff uses the summer to prepare for ''the onslaught in the fall,'' according to their manager.

For all programs, the department prefers the classes to be as small as possible. The desired maximum number of students is one hundred. All programs involve group participation and include a question and answer period. Most have slide presentations put together by the consumer relations staff. Tours of JCP&L plants are also conducted by community relations representatives and retired employees of the company.

The length of the programs vary. For kindergarten through third grade, the program is never more than twenty minutes. For grades four through twelve, the programs are forty-five minutes or correspond to the regular class period in the school. Adult day programs are usually twenty minutes plus a question and answer period that can last up to one hour. Evening programs tend to be longer. A special dialogue program is held for senior citizens with a five to seven minute presentation on energy conservation followed by questions and answers. This session can go on for two or three hours, which happens about 75 percent of the time.

Materials are distributed at all programs. Materials used primarily with residential customers and school groups include a folder containing fourteen pamphlets on such topics as: helpful hints on the wise use of electricity, Thomas Edison, nuclear energy, solar energy, a-b-c's of electricity, and others. Another set of materials is used with commercial and industrial customers. Included are specialized pamphlets such as "Cost and Energy Savings Opportunities with Heating, Air-Conditioning and Lighting Systems in Schools." Each pamphlet in this series states how to get maximum performance from particular equipment, such as electric refrigeration units, electric fry kettles, and electric boilers.

All JCP&L's training and materials are free with the exception of one program entitled "Energy Management Action Course." This course, which is conducted by the consumer services department, is designed to provide an enrollee with the techniques and methods for retrofitting energy systems in existing industrial, commercial, and institutional buildings. The emphasis is on practical approaches that can result in significant increases in energy efficiency throughout all systems and for all forms of energy. Course participants receive instruction on how to complete an energy audit using their own buildings as a course project. They are then shown how to analyze the audit and determine low-cost efficiency moves that can be instituted by their own firms internally. In addition, participants are taught how to evaluate moderate cost and capital-intensive energy efficiency options that may require outside services, how to secure estimates for these options, and how to determine payback considerations.

This course is offered twice each year. In the fall it is offered at JCP&L's Morristown facility (northern New Jersey) and in the spring, at the company's Lakewood facility in southern New Jersey. The basic course is designed for units of two and one-half hours each. The course is conducted one afternoon per week for five consecutive weeks. A complete textbook for study and reference is supplied to each participant. Lecture, group discussion, demonstration, product literature, and audiovisual presentations are all used in the course. Homework assignments are based upon actual energy operations of the participant's own building. The course is evaluated by a participant critique. Upon completion of the course there is a graduation dinner where diplomas are awarded. The fee for this course in 1980 was $75. The manager of consumer services stated that the fee covers JCP&L's out-of-pocket expenses. It does not cover overhead expenses, such as the cost of maintaining the classroom.

Each class has about thirty persons and is taught by a person outside the company. Formerly, the course was taught by JCP&L employees. This arrangement was changed because JCP&L employees lacked the time necessary for course preparation, and they were not experienced teachers. The present instructor is a consulting engineer specializing in the field of energy management. He approached JCP&L about teaching the course, and they accepted his proposition. The manager of consumer services stated that the evaluations for the course have improved since this outside person started teaching it.

The basic course was developed by the Electrification Council of the Edison Electric Institute, a private group that markets programs to utilities and colleges. JCP&L bought the course from them, which includes an instructor's manual, student text, and audiovisual material. The manual contains everything needed to run the course, including sample letters to participants and instructions on how to set up a graduation dinner for the participants and their supervisors. This is the only program that is formally evaluated. The students are asked to evaluate the course and the instructor at the close of the course. They are also asked to indicate how the course was beneficial to them.

The manager of consumer services stated that the company can also indirectly evaluate its customer education by their consumer survey. JCP&L surveys their residential customers once every two years. The purpose of the survey is threefold: to get demographics, to find out what people are doing in energy conservation, and to suggest what individuals might do to conserve energy. The rationale for saying that this information tells the company whether or not their customer training is effective is that if the customers are consciously conserving energy, it can be at least partially attributed to company programs or to the literature the company distributes.

The manager of consumer services noted several major problems and barriers JCP&L encounters in their customer training activities. One problem is the lack of customer interest in energy conservation alone. People want to conserve energy but they also want to see a monetary return for it. Also, many people will resist conserving if it means a significant change in their lifestyle. After the Arab oil embargo, electric consumption dropped off significantly. However, once consumers became accustomed to the higher prices, consumption began to rise again, although at a slower rate than before the oil embargo.

Table 6.1
Change in average energy usage by residential customers by year
(weather adjusted).

Year	Percentage
1965-1973 (oil embargo)	7.2
1974	– 1.5
1975	2.3
1976	1.2
1977	.9
1978	.2
1979	2.9

A second problem is the restriction of funds and manpower. Realistically, JCP&L cannot devote all its funds and time to customer education. However, like any other company, JCP&L could do more given greater resources. JCP&L relies a great deal on the customers contacting them. They also use mass media contacts and depend on the customer seeing or hearing this information.

In some programs, JCP&L representatives stress the importance of nuclear energy. The consumer relations manager stated, "We're not pro nuclear, we're pro energy." She further stated that forty-nine cents of every dollar JCP&L spent in 1980 went for fuel to make electricity and their average cost of fuel for the twelve month period ending December 1980 was:

		% Energy
Nuclear	$ .00385/kilowatt hour	14
Coal	$ .01039/kilowatt hour	13
Oil	$ .06167/kilowatt hour	8
Gas	$ .04110/kilowatt hour	8
Purchased	$ .03613/kilowatt hour	57
Average Cost	$.003136/kilowatt hour	100

Therefore, from a cost perspective, it seems logical that JCP&L stress the importance of nuclear energy.

In summary, JCP&L has a large, organized customer education program. The people involved seem to be enthusiastic and relay this to participants in their programs. They view customer education as a necessary thing to do. JCP&L spends a lot more money on customer education than required by law, for none of their commercial and industrial work is required. Conservation is not viewed as a threat to their profits. New Jersey is a densely populated state with increasingly greater numbers of people to serve.

Since the mid–1960s JCP&L has had an increase of approximately 13,000 residential customers per year. So, even if average usage per customer decreases, it will be compensated for by an increase in the number of customers. Taken one step further we can say that decreased usage could decrease the likelihood of having to build new plants, which is very expensive, thereby slowing the need for rate increases.

7
Merrill Lynch, Pierce, Fenner & Smith, Inc.

Merrill Lynch, Pierce, Fenner & Smith, Inc. is the largest securities firm in the United States. It offers a variety of financial services as a broker and dealer in securities, options, commodity futures contracts, and mutual funds, and as an investment banking firm. By the end of 1980, eight thousand account executives in four hundred offices were offering their securities services to 2.4 million active customer accounts.

Along with offering a broad range of financial services to its customers, Merrill Lynch sponsors a wide range of programs to educate and inform the investing public. The company calls this customer education program public education, since almost all its educational activities are made available to the general public. This is because those persons who would be interested in the seminars and are not already customers are potential customers.

One aspect of Merrill Lynch's public education program is publishing educational and informational pamphlets and brochures on a variety of financial topics. A few sample titles are: "How to Read a Financial Report," "Understanding Options," "Investing in Municipal Bonds for Tax-Free Income," "What Is Margin?" and "How Over-the-Counter Securities Are Traded." These publications are used by corporations, universities, and other educational institutions for their training programs and curricula. The publications are free of charge to Merrill Lynch customers and the general public. They are usually available from local offices upon request. Occasionally, a local office will advertise one of these free publications in a local newspaper with a coupon to send in to receive the publication.

Merrill Lynch also sponsors formal organized learning activities. In 1979, eighteen hundred seminars and forums designed to educate all levels of investors, from the beginner to the sophisticated, were conducted. In addition, Merrill Lynch sponsored large promotions on timely subjects in large cities throughout the country. Merrill Lynch has also sponsored some unique programs. These include an investment seminar in 1979 in New York City's Madison Square Garden that was transmitted via satellite to twenty cities throughout the United States, including Anchorage and Honolulu. Merrill Lynch makes special efforts to reach female investors. Twenty-three thousand women attended seminars on basic investing and money management in 1979. Additionally, Merrill Lynch published a special forty page booklet for women called "You and Your Money—A Financial Handbook for Women."

The formal organized learning activities at Merrill Lynch are a decentralized function. However, there is one person at corporate headquarters in New York, an investor information specialist, whose full-time job is customer education. She is a member of the Advertising Department. Her function is to do concept development, similar to that of an in-house consulting firm. She works with an idea and brings in specialists to develop a total package for a customer seminar. She then distributes the package to the local offices that request it. In this way, the corporate staff gives assistance to any local office that asks for it. They distribute their approved seminar kits, which are sample kits on how to conduct a particular seminar. A kit includes a sample letter of invitation, audiovisual material, advertising information, and a script for the instructor to follow. Scripts are developed by free-lance professional writers. The audiovisual material is developed by professional graphics people inside or outside the company. Merrill Lynch issues fifteen to twenty different seminar kits each year. In addition, someone from corporate headquarters will work with a local office to develop a seminar kit if one does not exist on the desired subject.

All seminars have to be approved by corporate headquarters to be certain the seminar meets Merrill Lynch standard legal requirements. The New York Stock Exchange has rules for educational activities sponsored by member organizations like Merrill Lynch. According to a Securities and Exchange Commission staff attorney interviewed, rule 405 of the New York Stock Exchange is the "Know Your Customer" rule. Under this rule, a broker is allowed only to recommend an investment that is suitable for the customer. An impact of this generalized rule is that a broker is not allowed to discuss a specific investment during an educational activity, because the broker would not know the customers or potential customers and therefore would not know what would be suitable for them.

If a local office does not contact the corporate office for assistance in planning or implementing an educational activity, the only record that Merrill Lynch has of these activities is a copy of a form entitled "Report of Speaking Activity." It is a requirement of the New York Stock Exchange under paragraph 2478 of the New York Stock Exchange Rules to complete this form whenever a speaking activity takes place. One copy is filed with the advertising department at Merrill Lynch, and the other copy is filed with the local office. The New York Stock Exchange requires that this report be kept on file for three years at Merrill Lynch and be available to the exchange upon request. This report should contain the following information for each speaking assignment: the name of the sponsoring group, its presiding officer (or program chairman) and his or her mailing address, the subject discussed, the date, approximate attendance, and the speaker's name. The investor information specialist at Merrill Lynch indicated that on the average she received thirty to forty of these reports each week in 1980.

In addition to the requirement of record maintenance discussed above, a senior interpretive specialist at the New York Stock Exchange discussed the other standards for speaking activities required by the exchange as stated in the 1979 *New York Stock Exchange Interpretation Handbook* (p.4714):

Recommending Specific Securities: When member organization personnel speak before community groups, schools, etc., the talk should be broadly educational. Specific recommendations either in prepared remarks or in response to questions, are considered promotional and only appropriate if specifically requested by the sponsoring group. However, when a member organization sponsors its own lecture, recommendations are permissible *if* investment objectives, suitability and the appropriate provisions of paragraph 2474A are met, (e.g., there must be a reasonable basis for the recommendation, current prices must be given, applicable disclosure concerning market making or underwriting must be made, supporting information must be offered, etc.)

Specific Examples When Recommendations Are Prohibited: Specific examples may be cited to add clarity and interest to a talk, but not as a means of recommending selected securities.

Approval By Member Organization: A member, allied member or competent authorized delegate should approve the topic of each talk and be satisfied that the speaker is qualified to present the subject and is knowledgeable with respect to Exchange Standards.

Monitoring Speaking Activities: In addition to periodic reviews of investment literature, the Advertising and Literature Review Staff, on occasion, monitor speaking engagements by member organization personnel. This audit is usually conducted on a surprise basis.

Since customer education activities are decentralized, each office makes its own decisions on how many seminars to offer, which ones should be offered, where they should be held, and all the other particulars about the seminars. Most costs incurred have to be covered by the local offices, so the local office makes the decisions on how much money to spend and what to spend the money on. What each local office does, then, depends upon its interests and budget. However, the cost of publications and seminar kits is borne by the company. In addition, the cost of seminar advertising is split by the local and the corporate office.

Account executives (salespersons) teach the seminars offered by Merrill Lynch. The seminars primarily consist of lecture and discussion and a substantial amount of time devoted to questions and answers. Some account executives use audiovisual aids, including videotapes, which are usually supplied by corporate headquarters. The participants are a combination of customers and potential customers. One office indicated that the breakdown was in the neighborhood of one-third customers and two-thirds potential customers. It varies since the participants are usually respondents to newspaper ads or a direct mail campaign. Ads sometime appear in national newspapers such as the *New York Times* and the *Wall Street Journal,* but more often they appear in local newspapers. Local advertising is preferred because it is less expensive. Merrill Lynch offices also look for local people to attend the seminars.

Seminars are also given for clubs or organizations. In some cases, the organization contacts a Merrill Lynch office and requests a seminar on a particular topic; in other instances, an account executive contacts an organization and offers his services.

Frequently, seminars are held at Merrill Lynch offices. This is the most convenient arrangement for the account executives and the least expensive arrangement. Most of the large offices have a conference room that can be utilized for this purpose. If a room is not available at the office, a room at a local hotel is used. Costs incurred by using an outside facility are paid for by the local office.

Most Merrill Lynch seminars are not evaluated. Nor has the company done any study to determine whether or not these customer education activities are cost effective. The investor information specialist explained that Merrill Lynch has a ''paternalistic approach to customer education. Like the Sym's slogan 'an educated customer is our best customer,' we want to identify interest. The bottom line is whether or not business is generated through these activities. But you cannot tell right away. It can take someone one to five years to decide to invest. But the seminars do increase awareness about the benefits of investing.'' A similar comment was made by a local office vice president. He indicated that seminars are evaluated only by their success in developing customers.

Most seminars are scheduled for about one hour. I attended a seminar sponsored by one of the New York offices. The seminar was one in a series of ten advertised in the *New York Times* on March 1, 1981 and scheduled to take place between March 19 and May 19, 1981. The size of the ad was approximately two-thirds of two columns—an expensive advertisement—and it contained a registration form. The seminars were scheduled from 6:00 to 7:00 P.M. on each date indicated. However, because of an enormous response, each seminar was rescheduled two more times to include another evening session the same week and a 12:00 to 1:00 P.M. session on the originally scheduled date.

The seminar I attended was on tax investments. It was led by two Merrill Lynch tax investment specialists. This was the third scheduled session of this course and it was filled to capacity, approximately eighty-five people. At the start of the seminar, a short questionnaire was distributed asking for some basic personal information, the areas of tax investments that are of interest, and the amount of funds available for tax sheltered investments for 1981. One of the instructors indicated that the purpose of the form was to see which areas were of primary interest to the participants, implying that those areas would be stressed in the seminar. However, the form was not collected until after the seminar had ended. The format followed was:

General Introduction	5 minutes
Overview of Equipment Leasing	5 minutes
Overview of Oil and Gas	5 minutes
Overview of Movies	5 minutes
Overview of Real Estate	5 minutes
Short sales pitch for Merrill Lynch	5 minutes
Questions and Answers	30 minutes

The two instructors rotated speaking. The room was very small and very crowded. No handouts were distributed, although Merrill Lynch does publish a booklet on tax investments. The interest level was high. There was somewhat of a soft sell about the high quality reputation of Merrill Lynch. The instructors did not push tax investment/shelters, owing, perhaps, to the fact that they indicated they have more people interested in tax investment/shelters than they could accommodate.

In addition to this type of customer education seminar, the corporate customer education group conducts large so-called seminars for fifteen hundred to two thousand people two or three times each year. These programs are held in large cities around the country and are called promotions. The speakers are Merrill Lynch's chief researchers or economists from corporate headquarters. The primary objective of these seminars is to heighten the company image. For example, in 1981, corporate headquarters conducted a promotion on fixed income investments. Fifteen hundred people attended this seminar in Florida and one thousand attended in New Mexico. For these seminars, the corporate office does most of the work but receives assistance from the local office. These big promotions are taped and edited, revised, and packaged for local offices to use in their own seminars.

When asked if Merrill Lynch had an official policy on customer education, the investor information specialist interviewed replied, "Merrill Lynch, as the premier financial services organization, considers it their responsibility to provide free public education. Our only other corporate policy is to attempt to do our educating in a high quality manner. And, it's always free, except maybe lunch or substantial publications."

8

Hoffmann-LaRoche

Hoffmann-LaRoche, a privately owned Swiss-based company that employed approximately nine thousand people in the United States in 1980, is a pharmaceutical company. Through its Roche Chemical Division, it produces pure synthetic bulk vitamins. In 1980, the company supplied a wide variety of pharmaceutical and food customers with a broad line of bulk vitamins, particularly vitamins C and E. The company has eight facilities in New Jersey as well as facilities in six other states and is part of an affiliated group with facilities in twenty-eight other countries.

One group of Hoffmann-LaRoche customers is made up of companies that package the bulk vitamins in their final form, capsules and tablets. These are the companies to which Hoffmann-LaRoche mainly directs its extensive customer and consumer education program. This major customer education program is sponsored by the Roche Chemical Division and is entitled the vitamin education program (VEP).

The program originated as a result of a survey that revealed that consumers looked for specific nutritional information and had many misconceptions about vitamins. It was designed to increase customer knowledge and awareness of the benefits of good nutrition and the possible role of fortified foods and dietary supplements in insuring proper intakes of essential micronutrients. Elements of the program were designed to encourage and assist customers at the wholesale and retail levels to conduct their own educational programs. It was hoped that increased consumer knowledge of vitamin needs would broaden the base of retail customers for vitamin-related products. Hoffmann-LaRoche's customer education program is distinctive because its customers are not the ultimate consumers of the product.

I was not able to attend a vitamin education program session. However, I viewed a recent session, in its entirety, on videotape. I also looked at videotapes of a homemakers school, a vitamin nutrition information service conference, and a discussion led by Nutro, the robot. This case study will describe these and other aspects of Hoffmann-LaRoche's customer/consumer education program.

Vitamin Education Program

The VEP was initiated in 1976 as the culmination of an assignment given to the fine chemicals department. The assignment was to develop a communications plan that would enhance the market for fortified foods and for vitamin supplements through a program based on a solid scientific foundation. The fine chemicals department is one component of the Roche Chemical Division. The structure of the fine chemicals department and how this department fits into the organizational structure is shown in figure 8.1. The structure of the promotion group of the fine chemicals department, which conducts the customer and consumer education programs, is shown in figure 8.2.

The director of promotional planning and vitamin communications is in charge of the entire VEP. The manager of fine chemical promotion is in charge of all graphics and audiovisual material produced by Hoffmann-LaRoche or contracted to outside agencies. The trade promotion manager is responsible for organizing advertising campaigns and exhibits at conventions and conferences.

Since the program began, it has grown in scope and depth. The program's purpose was and continues to be to provide the market with scientifically sound information in the area of nutrition. The original focus of the program was to show the importance of good nutrition in general and vitamins in particular by conveying generic at-risk "messages." These dealt with everyday life situations, such as smoking, drinking, dieting, the Pill, and poor eating habits, that can affect an individual's vitamin needs or levels. The primary audience for these messages was women aged eighteen through forty-nine. The at-risk messages were communicated through consumer and professional advertisements and a variety of public relations activities. A number of customers also tagged on to the program. In a speech to customers during a VEP session, which I viewed on videotape, the director of vitamin communications stated, "Your activities have been the catalyst of this program's success."

The VEP is comprised of the following segments:

Educational Advertising—directed to consumers and professionals
Publicity—feature articles and news that communicates vitamin information
Public Service Television—national television spots on vitamins and nutrition
Public Service Radio—humorous messages that communicate vitamin information nationally
Spokesperson tour—national appearances on radio and television by a dietician and Nutro, the nutrition robot
Press Conferences—personal meetings with consumer and professional editors to discuss vitamins and nutrition
Vitamin Information Nutrition Service—a vitamin information resource for health communicators as a basis for the editorial material
Fitness 3—the newest program, which stresses fitness, nutrition, and health habits[1]

Aside from relaying vitamin and nutrition information to the public, the VEP attempts to convince wholesale customers to do more informative advertising. With this goal in mind, the com-

---

[1]Transcription of videotape appears by permission of Hoffmann-LaRoche, Inc.

pany supplies interested customers with a retail merchandising support kit. The kit contains quality reproduction artwork from the VEP, copy ideas and important data, order forms for available handout or ad-offer literature, and usage suggestions. The artwork is prepared by national advertising agencies and commercial art-

Figure 8.1.
The structure of the fine chemicals department and how this department fits into the Hoffmann-LaRoche organizational structure.

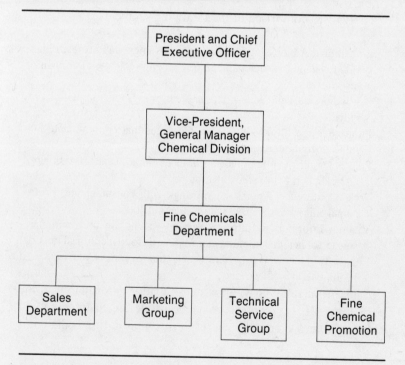

ists and photographers. Specific elements are often tested for consumer reactions before actual use. The data supplied contains current vitamin nutrition facts. The label on the kit states: ''Studies show consumers want to know. . . . Their interest in nutrition is at an all-time high. Research shows education helps sell.'' The available literature consists of booklets on vitamin nutrition prepared by Hoffmann-LaRoche and reviewed by nutritionists for accuracy.

Whenever the VEP adds a new program or changes direction, Hoffmann-LaRoche will hold an invitational meeting for its customers to describe and discuss these changes. These are called customer update presentations. To date, these have been held in three locations—New York, Chicago, and Los Angeles. There

Figure 8.2.
The structure of the Hoffmann-LaRoche fine chemicals promotion department.

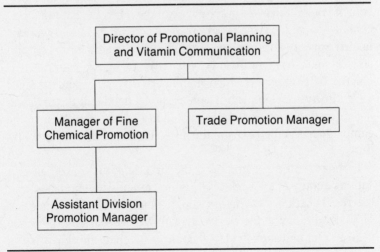

were four hundred attendees in New York, one hundred in Chicago, and two hundred in Los Angeles. The purpose of the program was to introduce a new aspect of the VEP called Fitness 3. The program also contained a review of the history of the VEP since 1976. This case will discuss this formal customer education presentation, including its content.

The content describes the consumer education components of the VEP. The program lasted about fifty-five minutes. The director of vitamin communications was speaker and narrator. His talk was supplemented by a slide show and videotapes of comments by some program participants, vitamin advisory board members, and various people discussing different aspects of the VEP. After a brief introduction by the director of vitamin communications, slides flashed on three tremendous screens depicting the different segments of the VEP since 1976. Accompanying the slides was music especially written for this program. The slides were prepared by an outside agency.

Afterwards, the director of vitamin communications discussed the results of the VEP to date by quoting statistics from a survey his department sent to its customers. He said: "Ninety-five percent of you said that you were aware of the VEP. Seventy-one percent of you said that the program and its communications were on target. Seventy-five percent of you have utilized the program resources and most significantly, your advertising expenditures, exclusive of newspapers, have increased fifty-nine percent since 1975. Forty-four percent of you acknowledged that the program has directly helped your sales and eighty-one percent believe the campaign has helped expand the market for vitamin supplementation."

In regard to the last comment, the director of vitamin communications quoted market research figures as showing an increase in the retail market for vitamin supplements of 180 percent since 1976. Additionally, the market growth was forecasted to continue at an accelerated annual rate. The reason given for this growth was that Americans are on a health kick; they are totally involved in the quest to look and feel good. One way they are doing this is by taking vitamin supplements. In 1980, vitamin supplements were a $1.7 billion market and growing, with 64 percent of the population defined as nonusers. Thus, only 36 percent of the 1980 population took some kind of vitamin supplement.

People take vitamins because they perceive them as part of their health equation. Therefore, the focus of the new VEP is the relationship between health and nutrition. Hoffmann-LaRoche conveyed this message by discussing two specific vitamins that are continually talked about—vitamin C and vitamin E. Each vitamin has advertisements that state an "essentiality message" for that vitamin and that use factual information to stress the need for the vitamin. All the ads have the same closing message: "Eat foods that are rich in these essential nutrients, look for fortified foods where you shop, and just to make sure, you can take a vitamin supplement." They also have the same tag line for the final impact: "Vitamins—something you can do for your health."

The advertisements appeared in Sunday newspaper supplements reaching 50 million people in 311 markets and were the vehicle for launching the vitamin C and vitamin E campaign. The ads also ran in seventeen magazines, including *Tennis, Sports Illustrated, Golf, Psychology Today, Newsweek, Time, National Geographic, Better Homes & Gardens, Readers Digest,* and *People.* Through these publications an additional 90 million people were reached. Vitamin education messages were also carried to health professionals, physicians, pharmacists, nurses, dieticians, and teachers through a variety of special interest journals. In addition, in 1981, Hoffmann-LaRoche brought the vitamin advertising to network television for the first time. These ads reached new segments of the population, as well as those people previously reached by the printed ads. These thirty-second television commercials were shown to Hoffmann-LaRoche customers during the VEP customer update presentation.

The director of vitamin communication stated that the entire advertising campaign for vitamins C and E reached 125 million people with direct factual information. This figure represented 124 placements, 56 on television and 68 in print—a four-fold increase over 1979. Hoffmann-LaRoche feels that the advertising is making an impact because of all the mail they are receiving. In many of the letters, people ask for advice on which vitamins to take for their particular ailment. For regulatory reasons, Hoffmann-LaRoche cannot and does not answer these questions.

Homemakers Schools

Another part of the VEP for retail customers is the homemakers schools. This is a private Madison, Wisconsin, based organization that has home economists conduct afternoon and evening meetings for rural homemakers. Classes are professionally produced educational demonstrations of recipes, products, homemaking ideas, and appliances. Meetings are free for the participants and last approximately two and one-half hours per session. The costs are covered by sponsors, including Hoffmann-LaRoche. The instructors demonstrate or discuss sponsors' products at their meetings. Since Hoffmann-LaRoche is a sponsor, the instructor uses literature and information supplied by the company to discuss the benefits of vitamins in general with an emphasis on vitamins C and E. Approximately 500,000 homemakers attend these sessions each year. In addition to the classes, the homemakers schools place extensive sponsor advertisements, supplied by Hoffmann-LaRoche, in local newspapers and on local radio and television. They also provide local retail outlets with the sponsors' window banners and shelf offers. In 1980, the homemakers schools reached approximately 14 million people by advertising the sponsors' products in 150 newspapers and 150 radio stations, and through displays in 3,000 supermarkets and pharmacies. Participants in these classes also receive a gift bag provided by Hoffmann-LaRoche that contains several informative booklets on vitamins. This segment of the VEP was illustrated, in the customer update presentation, by a videotape of a segment of a class in session.

Fitness 3 Program

A new segment of the VEP was launched in 1981 at a press conference in New York City. This was the Fitness 3 program. The three parts of the program are fitness, nutrition, and health. Fitness 3 was established when Hoffmann-LaRoche received the results of a national exercise/nutrition survey conducted for them by a large market research firm. The study indicated that Americans have a great deal of interest in fitness and quality of life. However, their perceptions of the benefits and meaning of exercise, a good diet, and health habits differ greatly from actual behavior in these areas. A Fitness 3 advisory council was established to make sure that the messages conveyed through the program are accurate and to communicate the messages in an authoritative manner. The advisory board members are leading authorities in the fields of physical activity, sports, and nutrition. They include a professor of epidemiology and public health medicine at a school of medicine, a medical doctor who is called the father of aerobics, since he is the founder and director of the aerobic center in Dallas, the head of a department of physical education at a major university, the head women's trainer at a major university, a professional football player, and a former professional basketball player and coach. The advisory council members all spoke a little about the program on videotape during the customer update presentation. At the time of this study, the program was just getting underway. However, a booklet including comprehensive information on the Fitness 3 program was published and advisory council members were scheduled to give lectures in at least eight cities throughout the United States on this program.

Vitamin Nutrition Information Service

Another aspect of the VEP discussed at the customer update presentation was the vitamin nutrition information service (VNIS) launched in 1979. The mission of this program is to minimize nutrition misinformation by providing documented vitamin nutrition information and story ideas to health communicators, health editors, broadcasters, key government people, and influential professionals. The service sponsors invitational conferences to discuss vitamin issues. The service also issues position papers that respond to misinformation. Vitamin information is brought to over six thousand health communicators on a regular basis and they, in turn, convey the data to their consumer audience. To date, there have been three VNIS conferences. The first conference was held over a weekend in 1979 in Boca Raton, Florida, and was entitled "Vitamin Nutrition Issues." Another conference entitled "Balancing the Balanced Diet" was held one weekend in Port St. Lucie, Florida, in 1981. At both these conferences, there were only about thirty-five attendees. This preserves the intimate nature of the programs and provides substantial opportunity for questions and for face-to-face discussions both during formal programs and informal gatherings. Hoffmann-LaRoche covered all the conference expenses including the travel, food, and lodging for the participants. The third was a one-day conference held in New York City in 1980 entitled "Teenage Nutrition: Threat or Threshold to a Healthy Adult Life." At this conference, there were approximately one hundred attendees.

For each of these VNIS conferences, professionals in the health field delivered talks on the given topic. Care is always taken to provide speakers who have differing viewpoints so that a fair, well-balanced program is presented. After each set of papers, a question and answer period was held. Presentation summaries were published for each conference and sent to the six thousand persons on the VNIS mailing list and fine chemical department customers. This program was commented on by three health editors who attended the programs and three speakers in a videotaped presentation shown at the customer update presentation. The comments were favorable.

These conferences were evaluated by the participants at the close of the programs. The questions asked included:

1. What was your overall impression of today's seminar?
2. Do you feel the material presented will be useful to you in your health communication efforts?
3. Overall, how would you rate today's speakers? Is there anyone you would like to interview further?
4. Were the seminar arrangements convenient for you?
5. Would you attend seminars of this nature in the future?
6. Is there a particular topic you would like to see addressed at a future meeting?

A summary of all the evaluations, including comments, was printed and sent to the vitamin advisory board (VAB) members. The director of vitamin communications indicated in his cover letter, sent with the evaluation summary, a list of suggestions and guidelines for use in planning future seminars.

The person in charge of the VNIS program is a registered dietician and a consultant to Hoffmann-LaRoche. She has traveled throughout the country as a nutrition spokesperson for the company and has appeared on radio and television talk shows nationally. Her goal is to clarify misconceptions about vitamins and to relay information on the benefits of vitamins.

Nutro

Nutro is a five-feet, two-inch, 450-pound, metal robot. It was created, according to Hoffmann-LaRoche, in response to the growing national concern for proper nutrition, children's poor eating habits, the increasing demand for more accurate information on nutrition, and the lack of effective nutritional teaching materials. Nutro lectures, quizzes, and talks with expertise and enthusiasm about nutrition as a teacher's aid in classrooms throughout the country. A nutritionist, who also serves as Nutro's voice and memory bank, travels with him. This researcher viewed several of Nutro's presentations on videotape.

Hoffmann-LaRoche, along with an outside advertising agency, developed Nutro in response to an apparent demand for better nutrition education. The company commissioned the Response Analysis Corporation of Princeton, New Jersey, to evaluate the level of nutrition education in the schools today. The research was conducted among 750 students and 448 educators. The study found that the great majority of students (80 percent) and educators (75 percent) reported they were very interested in food and nutrition. However, they were not knowledgeable about the subject. The students and educators did not know many simple facts about foods and the nutritional components of key food products, and they also held some major misconceptions about vitamins. The survey also found that although the educators recognized the importance of improved nutritional information, 83 percent felt somewhat restricted in teaching nutrition because of the lack of teaching supplies and materials.

Nutro is a radio remote-controlled robot. Its voice is live and spontaneous, never programmed like a computer. Nutro's purpose is to teach children the importance of good nutrition and proper eating habits. Nutro has toured the country teaching children in schools and appearing on television talk shows and children's shows, and he has been "interviewed" by newspaper and television news reporters. Nutro began making appearances in October 1978 and has appeared on or in *Good Morning America, Romper Room, People Magazine, New York Post, Washington Post, Chicago Tribune,* and many local television shows, in addition to grade school classrooms in major cities throughout the country.

Nutro's classes last for about forty-five minutes to one hour. They usually begin with some teasing comments and a few robot jokes. Nutro then moves into a discussion of the importance of nutrition, balanced diets, the four basic food groups, and the various nutrients essential to body energy, growth development, and general health. Afterwards, Nutro answers questions. To aid its presentation, Nutro distributes hand-held nutrition decoders for each student. The decoder has a picture of Nutro and on one side lists twelve different vitamins and nutrients and the benefits and sources of these vitamins and nutrients, as well as the United States Recommended Daily Allowances. It also gives a definition of nutrition. On the other side of the decoder, nine food categories are listed with their corresponding nutritional contents and the recommended food units per day.

Evaluations of Nutro's classes are kept in a file at Hoffmann-LaRoche. One typical reaction to Nutro was given by a home economics teacher at a middle school in Ramsey, New Jersey. She said: "The entire program was fantastic. The audience participation was super. Nutro was like a cheerleader as he got the students to respond. The presentation was never dull since Nutro changed topics often. The program was one of the highlights of our school year."

Nutro's effectiveness in imparting proper nutrition information to grade schoolers was partially substantiated by the improvement the students showed in a nutrition quiz taken before and after Nutro's class. The average post-class score was 15 percent higher than the average preclass score and the students showed improvement in eleven of the nineteen questions on the quiz.

Other Activities

In 1981 Hoffmann-LaRoche sponsored five vitamin program segments for the *Health Field* television series run by Dr. Frank Field, the New York City health editor for NBC-TV. This program was syndicated in seventy-three markets. The show ran one-half hour daily for one week. The subjects were: "Nutrition for All Ages," "Dieting and Weight Loss," "All About Vitamins," "Cancer and Your Diet," and "Vitamins and Health." The schedule of dates and cities where these vitamin programs were aired in 1981 was sent to all customers.

Hoffmann-LaRoche also sends its customers memos indicating when VEP commercials will be aired, during which television show, the estimated audience size, and audience profile. In addition, customers are sent the story boards for the VEP television advertisements.

Hoffmann-LaRoche also sponsors a physician's professional program, comprised of communication activities to support the VEP. As part of the program, the company sponsors "white papers," articles that deal with a clinical area that involves the physician. The papers discuss the nutritional ramifications involved with a particular issue and provide a thorough bibliography and specific recommendations for adjunct nutrient therapy. Two such papers were published in 1980, with three additional papers scheduled in 1981. These white papers are run as advertisements in selected medical journals and distributed to physicians. Another part of this program is the support Hoffmann-LaRoche gives to the official American Medical Student Association publication, *Infusion*. A member of the vitamin advisory board writes a column called "Nutrition Notes" in this publication.

At the close of the customer update presentation, the director of vitamin communications stated: "We are committed to the vitamin education program and we have committed significantly more money starting in 1981 than we have in the past. It should help make a very successful campaign more successful for the benefit of all. By working together in the dissemination of these messages, we can get them to more people with far greater impact and far greater return to us all. Vitamin education is working. When this concept was initiated, the retail market for vitamin supplements was estimated between $500 and $700 million annually. The latest estimates puts the market around $1.7 billion. . . . We will stand beside you to supply these consumers with more responsible information that will lead to a greater understanding of their nutritional needs. Let us form a partnership in that growth."

The customer update presentation was videotaped and is available for customers to borrow. This was primarily done to reach Hoffmann-LaRoche's customers who were unable to attend.

Hoffmann-LaRoche is making every effort to encourage and help its customers to advertise their products, with the goal of increasing vitamin supplement sales. Hoffmann-LaRoche further promotes this goal by the massive consumer education program it conducts, consisting of organized learning and information giving. This program seems to have helped to increase the market for vitamin supplements. Although the budget for these programs was not made available, it is obvious by the scope and the quality of the programs that Hoffmann-LaRoche has committed a great deal of money to them in the hope that more and more people will use vitamins, thereby increasing sales of the bulk vitamins.

9
Findings and Conclusions

The questions this study sought to answer were:

1. What are the organization's objectives for customer educa- tion? Which of these objectives is most important under what circumstances? Is there one particular objective that is domi- nant for a particular kind of product?

2. What is the structure of customer education within a com- pany? What is the relationship of customer education to em- ployee education and to the sales function? How does the customer education function fit with other related company functions?

3. How is customer education financed? Are the costs for cus- tomer education included in the price of the product or charged separately? How are costs determined?

4. What educational methods and materials are used for cus- tomer education? How frequent is the use of each of these methods and under what circumstances and in what combi- nation are they likely to be employed?

5. Is customer education evaluated? To what extent? How? For what purpose?

6. What are the major problems, issues, and questions for fu- ture research?

Objectives for Customer Education

The case studies indicate that customer education is considered integral to marketing and sales. The primary objective for each customer education program studied, with the exception of JCP&L, was to aid the sales process in some way. JCP&L was the exception due to the nature of its product. The company has a captive clientele since customers cannot choose the company from which they buy their electricity. In addition, by law, the company cannot advocate the increased use of electricity. JCP&L must encourage energy conservation.

A secondary purpose for customer education at Digital, Varityper, and JCP&L was to reduce service calls. At classes sponsored by Digital and Varityper, simple, common problems that could occur when using the company's products were described and the solutions to these problems were explained. At JCP&L classes, the proper and safe use of electricity was explained to avoid possible problems.

Lusterman's (1977) statement that the purpose of customer education is primarily to teach skills and knowledge that are vital to the sale, maintenance, or use of the product holds true for each of the companies studied. Training is necessary to use the phototypesetters manufactured by Varityper, the computer hardware and software sold by Digital, and the medical diagnostic equipment produced by Ortho. Both Merrill Lynch and Hoffmann-LaRoche want to impart knowledge about the benefits of their products and services in order to increase their markets and sales. JCP&L disseminates knowledge on energy conservation and the proper and safe use of electricity.

McGuire (1973) indicated three purposes for customer education: to promote customer satisfaction, to help customers make better initial purchase decisions, and to increase public awareness of products and services. All six companies studied were interested in customer satisfaction, especially the companies where specific knowledge is necessary to utilize the product—Varityper, Ortho, and Digital. In the cases of Merrill Lynch, Varityper, and

Digital, McGuire's second purpose for customer education was significant. Because these three companies offered a wide range of products, it was especially important for the customer to purchase the product that best fulfilled his needs since this would increase his satisfaction with the purchase. Increasing public awareness of products and services was an important reason for the customer education activities sponsored by Merrill Lynch and Hoffmann-LaRoche. A representative for Merrill Lynch indicated that the company's primary reason for offering customer seminars was to increase awareness about the benefits of investing. At Hoffmann-LaRoche, the company's philosophy for its customer education program was that sales would increase through awareness of the benefits of vitamin supplements.

Increasing public awareness of their products was also important to Digital and Ortho. These companies tried to fulfill this objective by forming linkages with local schools. At Ortho, sales representatives lectured at schools that offered a curriculum in medical technology. The underlying goal was to acquaint students with Ortho products. Digital sponsored a minicomputer technology program with local colleges to train students for careers in computer service technology. Again, this program familiarized students with Digital equipment and also increased the number of people who were able to provide maintenance for Digital equipment.

Structure of Customer Education Units

Customer education is not usually a separately organized unit within the company and therefore tends to have low visibility. The exception to this was the educational services department at Digital and the former educational services department at Ortho. The case studies indicate that customer education was provided by different units within corporations. Digital and Varityper were the only companies that had a linkage with employee training. Customer training and employee training were both encompassed by the educational services department at Digital. However, the courses were segregated. On occasion, an employee attended a customer training course but a customer was never allowed to attend an employee course. Varityper had a similar arrangement.

All the companies studied, except JCP&L, related customer education to the sales function. This is not surprising, because the primary objective of these programs was to increase sales. At Varityper, the customer trainers gave demonstrations on the phototypesetting equipment for potential customers at the sales representatives' requests. At Ortho, the customer education personnel trained the sales representatives to give demonstrations. They also provided the sales representatives with lecture outlines, audiovisual material, hand-out material, and samples to work with. The primary connection between sales and customer education at Digital was the retail stores. These are facilities where customers can go to learn how a computer or word processor can help them in a cost-effective manner. In this instance, Digital used training strictly as a selling tool. All instruction given at Digital retail stores was provided by sales representatives and was the responsibility of the sales department. However, the educational services department wrote all the materials and prepared all the audiovisual presentations for these instructors.

At JCP&L, customer education was conducted by the consumer affairs group. No sales department existed at this company. However, the people who were formerly involved with sales were the personnel who visited homes and corporations to do energy audits and informally teach their customers about energy conservation. These people were in the consumer services department of the consumer affairs group. The more formal customer training was based out of the corporate communications department, which was also part of the consumer affairs group.

At Hoffmann-LaRoche, all customer education was based in the fine chemicals promotion department, which was affiliated with many outside advertising agencies and the Hoffmann-LaRoche marketing group. Merrill Lynch's customer training was directly affiliated with sales because most of the customer training was taught by account representatives, who were the equivalent of sales representatives.

Customer Education Finances

Training for potential and actual customers was free in most cases and a minimal fee was charged in other cases. The companies justified these expenses on the same basis that other sales expenses were justified. The cost of a certain amount of training given after the sale was included in the price of the product. Extra training, if requested by a customer, might entail an extra fee. Training that took place after the sale, which was termed ''free,'' actually was not free; the cost was included in the price of the product. However, the actual cost of the training was never calculated, except at Digital.

At Varityper, since most training was after the sale, the cost of the initial training was advertised as free. In actuality, it was built into the price of the phototypesetter. The marketing support representatives, who conducted the training, taught two of the customer's employees how to use the machine. Any fee for additional training was decided upon by the branch manager according to ''customer worthiness.'' If they decided to charge a fee, corporate headquarters suggested what the fee should be. Actual training costs for the company were not available.

Ortho's criterion for establishing fees for its customer education activities had to do with whether or not the training was related to Ortho products. Training directly related to use of Ortho products was free for customers and potential customers. Other courses had a minimal fee attached to them; a company representative estimated that 50 percent of this training was subsidized by Ortho. Most training material written and distributed by Ortho was free for customers, but there was a charge for those who were not customers. Everyone was charged a minimal fee for material that included samples; this fee covered only the cost of the samples.

At Digital, training for one person on the purchased equipment was included in the cost of the product. For additional training for this person, or for the training of more than one person, a fee was charged. Digital was the only company studied that indicated its customer education unit was a profit-making division of the company.

Most of JCP&L's customer training was free, except for the "Energy Management Action" course, for which a minimal fee was charged to cover out-of-pocket expenses. Home energy audits, an informal customer training program, also involved a minimal fee. At Hoffmann-LaRoche and Merrill Lynch, two companies where customer training was primarily offered to gain sales, all training was free to the customer. At Hoffmann-LaRoche, the costs were justified as advertising and promotion expenditures. At Merrill Lynch the costs were justified as sales expenses.

Evaluation of Customer Education Programs

The case studies, as well as the literature, indicate that customer education was thought to be effective even though formal evaluations were seldom conducted. Most companies equated well-attended customer education classes with effectiveness. Digital was the one company that tried to assess whether or not students were learning. This may be because the company had many professional educators on their staff. At Varityper, the customer training was not evaluated. However, the instructors evaluated the customer trainers in their train-the-trainer classes. The instructor discussed this evaluation with the trainee. Subsequently, a written report was sent to the trainees' branch manager. The trainees, however, did not evaluate their training.

Ortho did not evaluate its customer training classes either. When upper management asked its former customer training department, called educational services, to justify its existence and budget, the head of the department attempted an evaluation of the entire program. He looked at the customer accounts that showed an increase in sales during a particular time period. Then he separated these accounts into those where the customer received training and those where the customer did not receive any training. He found that the customer accounts that included training and sales increases outdid the accounts with sales increases and no training by 14 percent. Although this is not a tremendous differential, it was still considered meaningful. The Ortho sales representatives claimed that their efforts increased sales, not the efforts of the educational services department. This was perhaps the main reason for the minimal amount of evaluation conducted. No simple way had been determined to single out the effect of training on the primary objective—increased sales. Some of the programs that Ortho conducted before the reorganization that were not entirely related to Ortho products were evaluated by the participants at the close of the program. A company representative indicated that the other programs did not need to be evaluated because they were in great demand. Popularity, then, was equated with effectiveness.

Digital was the one company that maintained an elaborate evaluation of its programming, entitled the quality assurance program. The primary objective of the evaluation was to assess the learning itself, not how the learning affected sales. For many of the courses, students were tested before a course to ensure they had the necessary prerequisite knowledge. Tests were also administered during a course to make sure the students were learning. In addition, instructors fill out questionnaires as they observe each student while he or she was working on the computer. At the close of a course, each participant completed a student opinion form, and the instructor completed an instructor opinion form that assessed course effectiveness, the environment, and the materials used. These forms were analyzed at the local training center where the course took place. The results were fed into the computer to be summarized and sent to corporate headquarters. Detailed reports were also printed for the students and instructors.

At JCP&L the only customer training that was evaluated was the energy management course, because this was the only course for which there was a fee. It was also the only formal course offered by JCP&L. At Merrill Lynch there was no evaluation of customer education activities at all. The customer programs were judged only by their presumed success at increasing sales. At Hoffmann-LaRoche, the conferences that were part of its vitamin nutrition information service were evaluated by the participants. The questions asked in the evaluation questionnaire primarily dealt with the seminar's environment, such as location, and the usefulness of the information presented. Evaluations were summarized, printed, and sent to Hoffmann-LaRoche's vitamin advisory board members. Based on the evaluations, a representative from the department coordinating these seminars drew up a list of suggestions and guidelines for use in planning future seminars.

Methods and Materials Utilized During Customer Education Activities

The case studies indicate that customer education formats are highly varied and utilize many types of materials. At Varityper, most training was individual or in small groups of three or four. It was informal. The training was usually at the customer's facility, although it could also take place at a Varityper location. The actual training took three to seven days, depending upon the complexity of the system and the experience of the operators being trained. In addition, follow-up training was automatically offered at the end of four, eight, and twelve weeks. The training consisted primarily of demonstrations with the aid of the accompanying operating manuals.

Ortho's training consisted primarily of formal courses and workshops ranging from one day to one week. The size of the classes usually ranged between fifteen and twenty participants, with a minimum of twelve persons per class. Training took place at an Ortho facility or at a hospital. Short courses tended to be in-field; the longer courses tended to be held at an Ortho facility. During most training courses, individuals participated in the educational experience via case studies and actually working on samples. In addition, programs were comprised of lectures, discussions, and demonstrations. The programs utilized literature and educational aids developed by educational services. These included seminar reports, books, pamphlets, brochures, films, slides, charts, newsletters, and self-instructional packages.

Digital's extensive customer education program was comprised of three hundred different courses in seventeen languages. These were packaged as lecture/laboratory courses and self-paced instruction. Class size usually ranged from two to twenty persons, with an average of ten students. (However, class size had ranged from one to ninety students per class.) Training took place at the customer's facility or at a Digital training center. In 1979, 20 to 30 percent of the customer training took place at the customer's location. Course length ranged from two days to three weeks, with one week being the average length. Both self-paced instruction and the lecture/laboratory courses made extensive use of the computer so that the participants could receive hands-on training. Five hundred computer systems were made available for this purpose. In addition, the educational services group that provided this training also published a quarterly newsletter and wrote various publications to complement the training.

At JCP&L most customer education programs were relatively informal. The exception was the energy management course. The education conveyed during energy audits was one-on-one and totally based on individual need. The energy management course, taught twice each year, had approximately thirty students in each class. The other training classes, conducted by the corporate communications department, had any number of students, but most had approximately twenty participants. Except for the energy management course, which lasted for five days, customer classes usually lasted only a couple of hours. The classes were primarily comprised of a lecture and discussion, with a great deal of time spent on questions and answers. Class sessions often included audiovisual presentations, and booklets on different energy issues were usually distributed.

Customer education activities at Merrill Lynch were somewhat formal. Many seminars were only one hour in length. Almost all the seminars contained a short lecture followed by a lengthy question-and-answer period. Merrill Lynch publishes many booklets on the various aspects of personal finance and these were oftentimes distributed at the seminar. The seminar size was usually large, with fifty to one hundred participants in each class. Most of the time, seminars were held at Merrill Lynch facilities or facilities arranged for by Merrill Lynch. However, when a specific organization or school requested a seminar, the organization took care of all housekeeping arrangements, including the class location.

Hoffmann-LaRoche's customer education activities were also primarily formal. The predominant format followed was a lecture utilizing audiovisual material with a question-and-answer period. Most programs had many participants, usually over one hundred per program. Some programs were held in large cities throughout the United States in space rented from hotels. Others were held at resort hotels. The city programs tended to be for one day or a portion of a day. The programs held at resorts were usually held over a three-day period. The seminars held in the city had a larger number of participants than those held at resorts because of the cost. Probably because Hoffmann-LaRoche's program was strongly related to advertising, the company spent a lot of money on elaborate audiovisual presentations. In addition, extensive handouts were usually distributed.

How Customer Education Programs Are Staffed

Some companies maintain a separate staff for customer education activities, and other companies have personnel work part-time on customer education. However, most companies have both full- and part-time employees for this function. Varityper maintained a separate staff of personnel to teach customers how to use its products. These people were called marketing support representatives (MSRs). The MSRs were based in the various branch offices and were affiliated with the sales department. The staff maintained a high level of autonomy. The MSRs were all college educated but had varied backgrounds. They were young; an estimated average age was the late twenties. Others in the marketing department aided the MSRs by supplying them with some teaching material. Ortho had a separate staff for customer education located in the educational services department. Ortho's staff was comprised of medical technologists who seemed well versed in their field. These people not only coordinated their own teaching activities, but also wrote hand-out materials, articles, and self-instructional packages. Ortho also received assistance from persons outside the company; some outside professionals were used for teaching, and one course was coordinated with assistance from local universities. In addition, sales representatives conducted some training with the assistance of members of the educational services department.

Digital had a large, full-time customer education staff located in its educational services department. Approximately four hundred fifty professionals were involved in course development, production of outlines, graphs, and audiovisual materials, translating material into foreign languages, and monitoring quality. In addition, Digital employed five hundred fifty full-time instructors, all recruited from the ranks of school teachers. Many of the other professionals were from academia, and many held doctoral degrees in the field of education or computer science. Since Digital's education operation was so extensive, the company had training center managers and assistant managers at its twenty-five customer training centers and many nonprofessionals to assist the training operation.

At JCP&L, the instructor for the energy management course was an outside person hired for this purpose only. The other people involved in customer education were full-time employees of JCP&L. Four persons worked full time conducting customer education activities. An additional twenty-four persons devoted part of their time to customer education. The four full-time people had a home economics background. The twenty-four part-time people worked in different capacities at JCP&L and had varied backgrounds and specialties. They taught in customer education programs because they enjoyed it; they received no extra compensation for their involvement.

Merrill Lynch had only one full-time person involved in customer education. This person was located in the advertising department at corporate headquarters. She aided local offices in any way she could regarding their customer education activities. Merrill Lynch account executives were the instructors at almost all programs. However, at a major conference, a representative from corporate headquarters might instruct. Much of the material that was issued to assist the account executives in their presentations and many of the booklets published for Merrill Lynch were written by outside professionals commissioned for this purpose.

At Hoffmann-LaRoche, one small department, comprised of four professionals, had the responsibility for the company's customer education program. In addition, many outside agencies and professionals were employed on a part-time basis. Most of these professionals and agencies were hired to enhance the company's publicity efforts. The professionals primarily acted as spokespersons. They provided information endorsing the benefits of vitamins and nutrition. The agencies provided the needed artwork and graphics as well as much of the audiovisual material used in the customer education programs. A songwriter was also hired to write a song on nutrition to accompany an audiovisual presentation, and a professional singer was hired to record the song. In summary, many outside services were used, depending upon the situation and what was needed.

Problems and Issues

Several problems surfaced during the study of the six companies. Several company representatives expressed a need for more funds and human resources. This was not atypical. Most people believed they could do more given greater resources. Justifying an increased budget was a problem when the customer education units had not been able to show whether or not they were effective in terms of the objectives they set out to accomplish. Digital did not have this problem because its customer education unit was profit making. The other companies either partially or totally subsidized their customer training. These companies wanted to be shown that they would get increased benefits from increased allocations for customer education. For example, most companies offered customer education to aid the sales process. If this was the primary objective, then it should be shown that customer education did increase sales and that an increased investment in these activities would result in an even greater number of sales.

A second problem that surfaced was that customers do not always want to spend the time needed for training. This was a potential problem only when training was a necessity to effectively use the product involved. Companies were concerned about this because if customers did not use the product properly, they would be dissatisfied with it, which could in turn affect the product's reputation. Customer dissatisfaction could also be caused by a sales representative underselling a customer. This could easily happen when a company offered a product with several models that differed in sophistication or capacity. A sales representative, who is primarily interested in making a sale, might sell the customer a lower priced model that would not perform at the same level as the higher priced model. If the lower-priced model did not do all the things the customer expected it to do, the result would be customer dissatisfaction.

Another problem that came to light was that customer education instructors were not taught instructional techniques and were not familiar with the field of adult education, except at Digital. All the trainers seemed to be experienced in their field of expertise, but this was no guarantee that they could impart the necessary information in an effective manner. At Digital, all the instructors were recruited from the ranks of professional educators and, therefore,

were experienced instructors. In-service training in adult education would be beneficial for most customer trainers.

Another significant issue is the fact that some customer education activities were affected by agencies or people outside of the
company. For example, at Merrill Lynch, educational activities
were guided by the rules of the New York Stock Exchange and the
Securities and Exchange Commission. At JCP&L, customer education activities adhered to the guidelines set forth by the Public
Utilities Commission and the State of New Jersey Department of
Energy. Some of Ortho's customer education programs were affected by the policies of the American Society of Medical Technologists, since this organization offered continuing education
units for some of the courses offered by Ortho. Thus, to some extent, companies were often constrained in what they could do.

It is impossible to make sweeping generalizations from six case
studies. However, it is possible to point out some common characteristics that emerge from the cases. From this study several analytical categories for customer education activities emerge. The
first relates to the point of consummation of the sale. Customer
education can take place before or after a sale. In two companies,
Hoffmann-LaRoche and Merrill Lynch, it was possible for the education to be provided at either point in time. Thus, the training
could be for present customers and/or potential customers. At the
other companies studied, customer education was geared primarily for customers, which meant that training took place after the
sale was completed. When training is given before the sale, it
seems likely that it is provided to aid the sales process. When the
training is provided after the sale, it primarily aids the marketing
process. As Levitt (1960:50) points out:

> Selling focuses on the needs of the seller; marketing on the needs of
> the buyer. Selling is preoccupied with the seller's need to convert his
> product into cash; marketing with the idea of satisfying the needs of
> the customer by means of the product and the whole cluster of things
> associated with creating, delivering and finally consuming it.

When training is offered before the sale, with the purpose of increasing sales, the company offering the training could also be helping other similar companies. For example, when Hoffmann-LaRoche and Merrill Lynch offered their training activities, they had the potential of widening the market, in general, for their kind of product. Hoffmann-LaRoche was advocating the increased use of vitamins. The company's training efforts could have benefited other suppliers of bulk vitamins as well, but it should have benefited Hoffmann-LaRoche the most since it had the largest percentage of the market for bulk vitamins. The knowledge acquired at Merrill Lynch seminars could also have benefited other investment brokerage companies, since the education offered was of a general nature. A participant could easily have used the knowledge gained from Merrill Lynch to invest with a different brokerage firm.

Another category indigenous to customer education activities that emerged from the study relates to the type of customer a company has. One type is the retail or net consumer. This type of customer was serviced by all the companies studied except Hoffmann-LaRoche. The other type, which describes Hoffmann-LaRoche's customers, is the customer that is the distributor or the intermediary between the manufacturer or supplier and the consumer.

Customer education programs also differed in their level of formality. In chapter 1, a continuum for customer education programs was suggested. At one end of the continuum are informal activities that are typified by information giving, usually through printed materials such as instructions. At the other end of the continuum are formal instructional activities, which includes structured workshops and courses. Most customer education programs seem to fall between these two ends of the continuum. In the case studies, workshops were somewhat structured, but a good deal of the learning that took place depended upon who the participants were and the level of knowledge they brought to the classroom. This was because much of this training involved hands-on learning and demonstrations due to the practical skills orientation of the training.

Customer education programs are difficult to compare because the training is directly related to the product or service being offered. This differs from employee education, where very often the programs attempt to teach skills that are applicable to different types of companies. Thus, much employee skills training is generic, whereas customer training is usually very specific. This may mean that although there is a clear career track for trainers in employee education, there may not be one for customer educators, because companies mostly need people knowledgeable about a specific product. This may also explain, in part, why employee training has been studied to a much greater extent than customer training.

Summary of Findings

The purpose of a company's existence in our industrial society is to sell a product or service and earn a profit. The ultimate goal of many activities within a company, including customer education, is to aid this sales and marketing effort. Other objectives for customer education programs, such as increasing customer satisfaction and reducing service calls, are secondary.

Customer education is a field that has not been studied to any great extent primarily because this function does not usually exist as a separate unit within a company. In general, most customer education programs maintain a strong linkage with the sales or marketing function and a limited linkage with employee education.

Many customer education programs are free, most others charge only a minimal fee. This is probably because the training is necessary for the proper use of the product or service, or the primary purpose of the training is to increase sales. It appears that the actual cost of the training is built into the price of the product.

However, only Digital indicated that they knew what these actual costs were.

Customer education classes incorporate various methods and materials. Most classes utilize lecture/discussion and question-and-answer formats. The sessions are usually supplemented by audiovisual presentations and demonstrations and practice sessions, when appropriate. Ortho and Digital also had available self-instructional packages. In addition, most companies provide some written material to their participants. The instructors for these sessions tend to be experts in their own fields. The exception was Digital, where the instructors were professional educators. Evaluation of these programs, except at Digital, is either nonexistent or largely superficial. This is one of the reasons that companies do not devote greater resources to customer education activities. Customer education units have not been able to show whether or not they are effective in terms of the objectives they set out to accomplish.

Recommendations for Research and Practice

Customer education is an area of adult education that has not been studied to any significant extent. As an exploratory study, this inquiry sought to identify areas for future research and practice. The following topics stand out as areas that, if given attention, would greatly benefit the field of customer education.

A descriptive analysis of customer education activities in a particular industry or geographic area should be developed. Several studies might follow utilizing this information, such as a comparison of the customer education activities of companies that manufacture simple products to determine if there are relationships between the type of product and the variables related to customer education such as organization, financing, and instructional methods. It would also be interesting to know if there are relationships between the type of customer (retail or distributor) and these variables, as well as the relationship of the point of consummation of the sale to these variables.

A second area of customer education that needs attention is evaluation. It is extremely important for customer education personnel to be able to determine whether or not their programs are meeting the objectives they seek to achieve. This knowledge would help solve two major problems faced by many customer education units. First, it could be used to justify requests for greater resources. Second, it could be used to show customers why they should devote the time deemed necessary for training their personnel. Determining what the actual costs for the training are is also important as this would make cost-benefit analyses possible.

A third topic that needs to be addressed is the need for training in adult education for customer education trainers. Such professional development of personnel would be beneficial to any company involved in customer education. Since most companies have a small number of individuals assigned to customer education, it might be necessary to develop a linkage between an educational institution and several companies in the same geographic location to teach customer education personnel these necessary skills. The field of adult education contains a wealth of interesting and unexplored questions. Customer education is an especially rich area for future research.

Appendices

1. Company Information

   a. Company Name _____
      Division Name _____

   b. Type of business (*Check as many as applicable*)
      ____ retail
      ____ wholesale
      ____ manufacturing
      ____ service
      ____ transportation
      ____ communication or other public utility
      ____ other (*please specify*)

2. What percentage of your sales/services are made to the following?

   ____ general public
   ____ retail
   ____ wholesale
   ____ manufacturing

_____ service
_____ transportation
_____ communication or other public utility
_____ other (*please specify*)

3. What kind of information or training do you provide for your customers or potential customers? (*Check as many as applicable*)

_____ use of your product
_____ maintenance and/or service of your product
_____ general information related to the product
_____ general information *not* specifically related to the product
_____ none

4. What forms does your customer training take? (*Check as many as applicable*)

_____ one-on-one at customer location
_____ one-on-one at your location
_____ group training
_____ lecture
_____ demonstration
_____ simulation exercises
_____ audio-visual presentations
_____ product literature
_____ instructions and/or operating manual
_____ samples of products produced
_____ other (*please specify*)

5. How important are the following reasons for providing customer training?

V = very important   I = important
L = less important   N = not important

_____ use of product
_____ to increase sales
_____ product awareness
_____ to reduce service/maintenance calls
_____ public relations/community service
_____ feedback for new product development or new uses for product
_____ customer satisfaction (so they can get full use from the product)
_____ safety
_____ obligated by law
_____ other (*please specify*)

6. Do you evaluate the effectiveness of your customer training activities?

    _____ yes   _____ no
    If yes, please describe briefly how you do so.

7. How effective is your customer training for each of the purposes listed below?

    V = Very effective E = Effective I = Ineffective U = Uncertain N = Not applicable

    _____ use of product
    _____ to increase sales
    _____ product awareness
    _____ to reduce service/maintenance calls
    _____ public relations/community service
    _____ feedback for new product development or new uses for product
    _____ customer satisfaction
    _____ safety
    _____ obligated by law
    _____ other (*please specify*)

8. When do you provide customer training? (*Check one*)

    ____ before purchase of the product or service
    ____ after purchase of the product or service
    ____ both before and after purchase

9. Do you provide follow-up training?

    ____ no   ____ yes
    If yes, is it ____ automatically ____ on request ____ both

10. How are customer training costs financed? (*Check as many as applicable*)

    ____ inclusion in price of the product or service
    ____ separate charge for training
    ____ other (*please specify*)

11. Who does the customer training for your organization? (*Check as many as applicable*)

    ____ salespersons
    ____ separate customer training staff
    ____ company training or human resource development unit
    ____ other (*please specify*)
    If separate customer training staff, how many professionals are employed in this capacity?

12. Please describe the major problems and/or barriers you encounter in your customer training activities.

13. Further comments:

14. Name, title and address of person answering questionnaire:

Please enclose any literature on your customer training programs or services that may exemplify any of your answers.
Thank you for your cooperation.

Appendix B
A Computer-Managed Instruction
Package at Digital

The CMI package begins as follows:

Digital Equipment Corporation
Educational Services
Managed Instruction System

Please identify yourself by typing your code name below and then pressing the RETURN key. If you have not yet registered on this CMI system and selected a code name, just press the RETURN key without typing anything else.

Your code name?

A typical CMI test item:

Multiple Choice.

Type the letter of the alternative that BEST answers the question or completes the sentence in the item below.

Type SKIP if you don't know the answer (counted as incorrect).

Type QUIT if you must terminate this test before it is completed.

Type REVIEW if you would like to see the previous test item again.

Press the RETURN key after you type your answer.

Example

1. An END statement may appear
   A) anywhere in a BASIC program
   B) only in conjunction with a PRINT statement
   C) as the last statement in a BASIC program
   D) without a line number

Your answer? C
Correct

How a student is informed of his exact status in a CMI course:

Name: CMI System Demonstration
Course: The Basic Primer

Module Status

1. Posttest completed satisfactorily
2. Posttest completed satisfactorily
3. Pretest completed satisfactorily
   Posttest skipped
4. Posttest completed satisfactorily
5. Posttest tried, but not completed satisfactorily
6. Pretest tried but not completed satisfactorily
7. Not attempted
8. Not attempted
9. Not attempted
10. Not attempted
11. Not attempted
12. Not attempted
13. Not attempted
14. Not attempted
15. Not attempted
16. Not attempted

You have met the prerequisites for Modules 5 and 6. You should now be ready for the test on at least one of these modules.

Type one of these numbers to run the test for the corresponding module. If you would like to see a list of the module titles, type LIST. If you do not want to be tested now, type QUIT.

Your choice? list

Module 5—Numeric Functions
Module 6—Program Control

Your choice?

Appendix C
A Student Opinion Form
at Digital

Course Name: _____

Course Number: _____

Course Ending Date: _____

Training Center: _____

This student Opinion Form is designed to help Digital assure the quality and usefulness of its training courses. Please respond carefully and objectively as indicated below.

Complete the course information above. Do not write your name anywhere on this sheet.

The other side of this sheet consists of two sections: Background Information and Evaluation of Course. In the Evaluation of Course section you will find a list of numbered statements that may or may not describe your opinions about this course. Please indicate whether you agree or disagree with each statement by selecting the appropriate lettered box from the following choices:

SA = Strongly Agree
A = Agree
U = Undecided
D = Disagree
SD = Strongly Disagree
NA = Not Applicable

Select the one best answer for each item.

Use the soft lead pencil provided. Blacken completely the box for the answer you select. If you erase, do so completely. Do not make any stray marks on the sheet.

Please use the space below for additional comments or opinions about your training experience here at Digital.

Comments on Course Design and Resources:

Comments on Instructor:

Comments on Training Facility:

Please read directions. Select the one best answer.

Background Information

What is your relationship with Digital?

(a) customer
(b) employee
(c) other

What is your primary job area?

(a) hardware
(b) software
(c) management
(d) education
(e) other

How many years of experience have you had with computers?

(a) less than 1
(b) 1–3
(c) 4–6
(d) 7–9
(e) 10 or more

Did you meet all the stated prerequisites?

(a) Yes
(b) No

Why did you take this course?

(a) general interest
(b) required for current job
(c) required for new job
(d) to help get new position

What is your native language?

(a) English
(b) Spanish
(c) French
(d) German
(e) Italian
(f) Japanese
(g) Chinese
(h) Dutch
(i) Swedish
(j) other

Evaluation of Course

SA = Strongly Agree   A = Agree   U = Uncertain
D = Disagree   SD = Strongly Disagree   NA = Not Applicable

1. I learned a lot of valuable skills and information.
2. The course content met my expectations.

3. The course was well organized.
4. The course materials were easy to understand.
5. I needed all the information contained in the course materials.
6. The course emphasized the real job.
7. My test scores accurately reflected what I learned.
8. The lab exercises were useful for learning.
9. The instructor was very knowledgeable in the subject.
10. The instructor answered difficult questions easily.
11. The instructor's presentations were easy to understand.
12. The instructor made the course interesting.
13. The instructor managed class discussions well.
14. The instructor took the time to answer questions.
15. The instructor was patient and helpful.
16. The instructor emphasized the objectives of the course.
17. The instructor made effective use of the available time.
18. The training center provided all the services I needed.
19. My workspace in the classroom was comfortable.
20. The classroom was well laid out.
21. The lab was functionally laid out.
22. The lab time was adequate for this course.
23. My housing was satisfactory.
24. Please indicate your overall impression of this training experience.

E = Excellent   VG = Very Good   G = Good   F = Fair   P = Poor

Reprinted by permission of Digital Equipment Corporation.

Bibliography

Antuck, Alexander, and Charles Wittnam. "Educating Your Way Out of a Price Bind." *Industrial Marketing,* June 1965. pp. 112–15.

Becker, Howard S., and Blanche Geer. "Participant Observation and Interviewing: A Comparison." In Leon Festinger and Daniel Katz (eds.), *Research Methods in the Behavioral Sciences.* New York: Holt, Rinehart and Winston, 1966.

Bender, Paul S. *Design and Operation of Customer Service Systems.* New York: AMACOM, 1976.

Blain, Ray. "Here's a Nostalgic Look at Those Days When Telcos Gave the Orders." *Telephony's,* Sept. 27, 1976, pp. 24–25.

Bruyn, Severyn T. "The New Empiricists: The Participant Observer and Phenomenologist." In William J. Filstead (ed.), *Qualitative Methodology: Firsthand Involvement with the Social World.* Chicago: Markham Pub. Co., 1970.

Buckner, Leroy. *Customer Services.* New York: McGraw Hill, 1978.

Ciccolella, C. "Consumer Held at Fault in Most Appliance Bugs." *Merchandising Week,* Nov. 10, 1969, pp. 1, 17.

Clark, Burton R. *Adult Education in Transition: A Study of Institutional Insecurity.* Berkeley: University of California Press, 1968.

Courting the Customer after the Sale Is Made. *Business Week,* May 28, 1960, pp. 70–72.

"Educational Systems Firm Specializes in 'How to Do It.' " *Inland Printer/American Lithographer,* July 1976, pp. 52–54.

Espeland, Pamela. "Training Salespeople to Train Doctors to Train Patients." *Training,* Nov. 1977, pp. 26–27.

Fraser, Bryna Shore. *The Structure of Adult Learning Education and Training Opportunity in the United States.* Washington, D.C.: National Institute for Work and Learning, 1980.

Geiger, R. F. "Meeting to Turn Prospects into Customers." *Sales Management,* July 4, 1958, pp. 111–14.

Goldstein, Harold. *Training and Education by Industry.* Washington, D.C.: National Institute for Work and Learning, 1980.

"Helpful Selling: Workers Trained in Product Use." *Printers' Ink,* Mar. 7, 1958, p. 96.

Jones, H. F. "Back to School Plan for Buyers." *Iron Age,* Oct. 25, 1962, p. 75.

Kerlinger, Fred N. *Foundations of Behavioral Research.* New York: Holt, Rinehart and Winston, 1973.

Kodak's New Learning System. *Graphic Arts Monthly,* Jan. 1969, pp. 46–53.

Kotler, Philip. *Marketing Management: Analysis, Planning and Control.* Garden City, N.J.: Prentice-Hall, 1976.

Landsberger, Henry A. *Hawthorne Revisited.* Ithaca, N.Y.: Cornell University Press, 1968.

Larson, John W. "Educating the Customer: Distribution's Third Dimension." *Industrial Distribution,* Mar. 1968, pp. 51–54.

Levitt, Theodore. "Marketing Myopia." *Harvard Business Review,* July-Aug. 1960, pp. 45–56.

Lusterman, Seymour. *Education Is Industry.* New York: Conference Board, 1977.

McGuire, E. Patrick. *The Consumer Affairs Department: Organization and Functions.* New York: Conference Board, 1973.

"Making a Pitch in the Classroom." *Printers' Ink,* Feb. 9, 1962, pp. 57–58.

Mansur, Gary. "Continuing Education: Valuable Tool for Industrial Marketers." *Industrial Marketing,* Nov. 1977, pp. 64, 66.

Olsen, Kenneth. "Chief Executives Report on How Training and Development Pay Off in Their Organizations." *Training,* Oct. 1978, p. 35.

Pearsall, Marion. Participant Observation as Role and Method in Behavioral Research. In William J. Filstead (ed.), *Qualitative Methodology: Firsthand Involvement with the Social World.* Chicago: Markham Pub. Co., 1970.

"School 'Advertises' New Full-System Service." *Industry Week,* May 6, 1974, p. 49.

Selltiz, Claire; Lawrence S. Wrightsman; and Stuart W. Cook. *Research Methods in Social Relations.* New York: Holt, Rinehart and Winston, 1976.

"Small Firm Expects to Double Sales by Taking Knowhow to the Market Place." *Steel,* Aug. 30, 1965, pp. 58–59.

Smith, G. B. *Employer-Sponsored Recurrent Education in the United States: A Report on Recent Inquiries into Its Structure.* Stanford, Calif.: Institute for Research on Educational Finance and Governance, Stanford University, Nov. 1980. (Project Report No. 80-A14)

"This Company Trains Its Customers Before They Buy." *Training,* Feb. 1981, pp. 50–51.

Wagner, Alan P. *An Inventory of Post-Compulsory Education and Training Programs in the U.S. and Sources of Support.* Stanford, Calif.: Institute for Research on Educational Finance and Governance, Stanford University, Nov. 1980. (Project Report No. 80-A13)

"Women Are Sent to Train Buyers of Photosetters." *Editor and Publisher,* July 27, 1974, p. 21.

"Worthington Keeps Classroom Busy." *Sales Management,* Sept. 18, 1964, pp. 161–63.

Zelditch, Morris Jr. "Some Methodological Problems of Field Studies." In William J. Filstead (ed.), *Qualitative Methodology: Firsthand Involvement with the Social World.* Chicago: Markham Pub. Co., 1970.

Index